THE
NORDSTROM
WAY to
Customer Service
Excellence

Also by Robert Spector

The Nordstrom Way:
The Inside Story of America's Number One Customer
Service Company

Lessons from the Nordstrom Way:
How Companies Are Emulating the #1 Customer Service Company

Amazon.com: Get Big Fast
Inside the Revolutionary Business Model That Changed the World

Anytime, Anywhere:
How the Best Bricks-and-Clicks Businesses Deliver
Seamless Service to Their Customers

Category Killers:
The Retail Revolution and Its Impact on Consumer Culture

THE
NORDSTROM
WAY to
Customer Service
Excellence

A HANDBOOK FOR IMPLEMENTING GREAT SERVICE IN YOUR ORGANIZATION

ROBERT SPECTOR AND PATRICK McCARTHY

WILEY

John Wiley & Sons, Inc.

Published by John Wiley & Sons, Inc., Hoboken, New Jersey.
Published simultaneously in Canada.

For general information on our other products and services please contact our Customer Care Department within the United States at (800) 762-2974, outside the United States at (317) 572-3993 or fax (317) 572-4002.

Wiley also publishes its books in a variety of electronic formats. Some content that appears in print may not be available in electronic books. For more information about Wiley products, visit our web site at www.wiley.com.

Library of Congress Cataloging-in-Publication Data:

Spector, Robert, 1947-
    The Nordstrom way to customer service excellence : a handbook for implementing great service in your organization / Robert Spector and Patrick D. McCarthy.
        p.   cm.
    ISBN 0-471-70286-2 (pbk.)
    1. Customer services—United States—Handbooks, manuals, etc.   2. Nordstrom (Firm)—Management.   3. Department stores—United States—Management.   I. McCarthy, Patrick D.   II. Title.
    HF5415.5.S626785 2005
    658.8′12—dc22

                                                    2004028848

Printed in the United States of America.

10   9   8   7   6   5   4   3   2   1

In loving memory of my parents,
Fred and Florence Spector,
who taught me The Spector Way:
Work hard, be good, do well.

R. S.

In memory of Ray Black,
who first showed me The Nordstrom Way

P. McC.

Acknowledgments

The names on an author's page cannot accurately reflect the vast number of people who helped make this book possible. As *The Nordstrom Way* has gone through several versions—including two hardcover editions—more and more people have made vital contributions.

For the original book, deep and heartfelt thanks to the following:

- Pat McCarthy for his belief in the Nordstrom way of doing business.
- Bruce Nordstrom, Jim Nordstrom, John Nordstrom, and Jack McMillan for their cooperation and trust, and for the use of two privately published family histories, *The Immigrant in 1887* by John W. Nordstrom, and *A Winning Team: The Story of Everett, Elmer & Lloyd Nordstrom* by Elmer Nordstrom.
- Elmer Nordstrom, John Whitacre, Ray Johnson, Jammie Baugh, Len Kuntz, Barden Erickson, David Lindsey, Patrick Kennedy, Bob Middlemas, Van Mensah, David Butler, Kellie Tormey, and all the Nordstrom salespeople and managers who put a human face on the company.
- Betsy Sanders for her thoughtful reading of the manuscript.

For this book, I would like to thank:

- Bruce, Blake, Pete, and Erik Nordstrom for sharing their insights in interviews with me.

ACKNOWLEDGMENTS

- My deepest appreciation to Brooke White of Nordstrom for her invaluable help in ensuring the integrity and accuracy of this manuscript. She responded to every request with speed, thoroughness, and good humor. Thanks also to Keli Fox and Jeanne McKay.
- Richard Narramore, my editor at John Wiley & Sons, shepherded this project with the utmost professionalism and gave it an exciting new format for the twenty-first century.
- Elizabeth Wales is the best agent (and friend) any author could ask for.
- My wife Marybeth Spector sustains me every day in every way and is the ideal spouse for an author—at least this one.

ROBERT SPECTOR
Seattle, Washington

Contents

Introduction

Soon after Nordstrom opened a mammoth 330,000-square-foot store in downtown San Francisco, a man purchased a dress shirt at the Emporium, a competing department store that was then adjacent to Nordstrom on Market Street, south of Union Square. As he headed toward the exit, the sales clerk suddenly called out to the customer: "Wait! Stop!"

The puzzled customer wondered what the trouble was.

"Can I have your bag back?" pleaded the clerk. The compliant shopper immediately handed the bag to the clerk, who proceeded to reach in, fish out the sales slip and scribble a quick "thank you" on it. "Ever since Nordstrom came to San Francisco," he complained, as he returned the bag to the customer, "we have to do that."

Seven years later, the Emporium was no more.

Fast forward to 2004. A female customer calls the Nordstrom store in Salem, Oregon. She had driven past the mall and had discovered when she got home that one of her hubcaps had fallen off. "Was there anyone in Nordstrom," she asked, "who could check the road that ran past the mall to see if my hubcap was there?" A Nordstrom employee did just that, found the hubcap, brought it back to the store, washed it, and notified the customer, who came in to pick it up.

"We love that story," said Pete Nordstrom, executive vice president of the company and president of its full-line stores, "because it means people don't just think of Nordstrom for buying things, they think of us as a place where they can find solutions."

Becoming the Nordstrom of Your Industry_____

At a time when *customer service* has become a core competitive advantage for every kind of business, the Nordstrom department store chain is the standard against which other companies and organizations privately (and often publicly) measure themselves. Nordstrom has long been a popular subject for study among authors of customer service books and educators at business graduate schools such as Harvard and Wharton. *Roll Call,* the newspaper of Capitol Hill, once advised press aides for U.S. congressmen to use the "Nordstrom approach" when trying to sell producers of political talk-shows on the benefits of booking their bosses. The *New York Times Magazine* quoted a minister in Bel Air, California, who told his congregation in a Sunday sermon that Nordstrom "carries out the call of the gospel in ways more consistent and caring than we sometimes do in the church."

Businesses of every kind strive to become the "the Nordstrom" of their industry. A quick search on Google found that the *San Diego Union* called Recreational Equipment Inc. "the Nordstrom of sporting goods stores" and *Specialty Foods* magazine described A Southern Season, a store in Chapel Hill, North Carolina, as "the Nordstrom of specialty food." Marty Rodriguez, a top broker for Century 21, once told *Fast Company,* "I want people to think of me as the Nordstrom of real estate." A dean at Fullerton College in California vowed to create "the Nordstrom of Admissions and Records." According to the *Denver Post,* the University of Colorado Hospital installed a baby grand piano in the lobby and began advertising itself as "The Nordstrom of Hospitals."

You can find similar comparisons in yoga videos, office furniture, public libraries, construction supply distribution, hot tubs, dental offices, pet stores, thermal rolls, garbage collection, foundries, workplace giving, doors and windows, and contract consulting.

Even Nordstrom uses this metaphor. In describing the company's Nordstrom Rack division of clearance stores, Blake Nordstrom said, "We like to think that the Rack is the Nordstrom of the discount world."

So, what does it mean to be the Nordstrom of your industry? The obvious answer is it means you have a unique commitment to customer service. How can an organization create a culture and atmosphere to provide "Nordstrom-like" service? This book answers those questions.

What Makes Nordstrom Unique?

The chain, which is geared toward middle-to-upper income women and men, offers its customers attractive stores, with a large, varied, and competitively priced inventory of shoes, apparel, accessories, and cosmetics, and a liberal return policy. But many stores do that—at least to varying degrees.

What makes Nordstrom unique is its culture of motivated, empowered employees, each with an entrepreneurial spirit. Nordstrom encourages, preaches, demands, and expects individual initiative from these people who are on the frontlines; people who have the freedom to generate their own ideas (rather than wait for an edict from above) and to promote fashion trends that are characteristic of that store and region of the country. The best Nordstrom sales associates will do virtually everything they can to make sure a shopper leaves the store a satisfied customer.

After all is said and done, the simplest explanation for what makes Nordstrom Nordstrom is that Nordstrom salespeople put themselves in the shoes of the customer. They do whatever they can to make life easier for their customers.

All of us are experts on customer service because all of us—at one point of the day or another—are customers. We know good service when we see it, and we know bad service when we see it. You don't have to read a book to have it explained to you.

But a funny thing happens to people when they are in the position of having to *give* service as opposed to getting service. Suddenly, they forget about the Golden Rule, they forget about empathy, they forget about the customer. When they are on the other side of the sales counter or the telephone or the front desk or the reception area, they think about the rules, the process, the manual, the bureaucracy, the way it's always been done. That's a recipe for terrible service. All of us customers only care about who is going to take care of us; who is going to make our life easier. That's where Nordstrom comes in. Nordstrom people will do whatever it takes (within reason, of course) to take care of the customer.

When you discuss customer service with members of the Nordstrom family, they frequently use a word that one rarely hears in American business: *humble*.

"You need to be humble to do service," said Erik Nordstrom. "The moment you think you're really good at it is when you're not really good at it. If you are connected to the customer, the customer keeps you humble because we're not perfect at it. If you are really looking to the customer, if you're really sensitive to the customer, and sensitive to the people on the frontline, you are aware of your shortcomings. That keeps us focused on the things that are necessary in order to give customer service."

When my book *The Nordstrom Way* was first published in 1995, it struck a chord with many companies in a variety of industries. Almost 100,000 copies and a second edition later, it continues to serve as an inspiration for many different types of businesses.

This book combines elements of *The Nordstrom Way* (particularly the brief history of the company) and a follow-up book *Lessons from The Nordstrom Way: How Companies Are Emulating the #1 Customer Service Company.* The latter book showed how other companies in other industries were giving Nordstrom-like service. (One of those featured companies, Continental Airlines, had been led by chairman and CEO Gordon Bethune, who retired on December 31, 2004. Bethune is identified throughout this book as the former chairman and CEO, however, it was his policies, leadership, and personality that shaped the company.) This book expands on the principles that were laid out in *Lessons,* and also adds implementation and training resources to help your organization become the Nordstrom of your industry.

The Nordstrom Way to Customer Service Excellence is divided into three sections.

■ *Part I: What Managers Can Do to Create Nordstrom-Style Service* looks at how an organization creates an identifiable and sustainable culture the way Nordstrom has done it. Nothing can be accomplished without the culture. Also in this section, we explore how organizations can create "an inviting place" for their customers, whether in person, online or on the telephone; and how organizations can provide their customers with a variety of choices to satisfy customers' needs.

- *Part II: What Supervisors Can Do to Create Nordstrom-Style Service* examines the area of influence of the people closest to the employees. These responsibilities include hiring the right people, then empowering, managing, mentoring, praising, rewarding, and retaining those people. At Nordstrom, frontline managers have the most important job in the company because they do more than anyone else to transmit the atmosphere and the culture to frontline employees.
- *Part III: What Employees Can Do to Create Nordstrom-Style Service* explores the role of employees in giving great customer service, including developing and maintaining personal relationships, and encouraging both teamwork and individual achievement among their peers.

Nordstrom, as I always tell my audiences, is not the perfect company. The perfect company has yet to be invented. In fact, in the late 1990s, Nordstrom began to experience problems, as sales dropped at stores opened at least one year (a key indicator in retailing) and the stock fell as well. The opinion of the media was summed up in a March 24, 1997 *Time* magazine double-page article that was headlined "Losing Its Luster." It was accompanied by a color photograph of a crushed Nordstrom gift box, wrapped in tattered ribbon. During this period, Nordstrom suffered through what might be called a crisis of confidence. The company spent millions of dollars on consultants.

By the fall of 2000, the Nordstrom board was looking for new leadership. Although several well-known outside retail executives were interested in taking over the helm, the board selected Blake Nordstrom, then 39, and president of the company's Nordstrom Rack clearance store division, to became president of the company. Like their grandfather, father, uncles, and cousins, Blake and his brothers Pete and Erik began working in the store as young boys, sweeping the floor and stocking merchandise at age 13. They worked their way up from selling shoes on the floor to attaining executive positions. Pete became executive vice president of the company and president of the full-line stores, and Erik was named vice-president of full-line stores. Their father, Bruce, then 66, returned as chairman, a position he shared with two cousins and a cousin-in-law until they all stepped down in 1995. After a failed period of nonfamily management, the Nordstrom family was back in charge of the company. Although some analysts were disappointed by the selection of Blake Nordstrom, the choice was cheered by Nordstrom insiders, from frontline salespeople to longtime managers, as a signal that the Nordstrom family was ready to rejuvenate the company's unique culture.

Blake, Pete, Erik, and Bruce toured stores, met with thousands of Pacesetters (top salespeople) over a six-week period, and were told that the company seemed to have lost confidence in its sales leaders' ability to inform management of problems on the frontlines. Salespeople "felt maybe we didn't trust them anymore and we weren't listening to them, that we didn't value them as much," said Blake, who added that the old policy was "bottom up management—where managers were there to facilitate sales staff. But the company now had bosses who said 'I am the manager and I know all the answers.'"

"At the end, I felt strangely invigorated," said Bruce. "These are amazing folks. They were a little ticked off and certainly had things to say. I felt so good about the amount of input I got."

By going back to the basics, Nordstrom turned things around. In 2004, the company recorded its fourth straight year of improved sales and profits. The company continues to be the most sought-after anchor store for mall developers because no other anchor has the power to draw such a broad cross-section of consumers. On August 19, 2004, a headline in the *Wall Street Journal* announced "Nordstrom Regains Its Luster."

With the help of this book, and the Nordstrom model, your organization can create its own service "luster" by satisfying and delighting your customers.

WHAT MANAGERS CAN DO TO CREATE NORDSTROM-STYLE SERVICE

Part I, "What Managers Can Do," examines the influence of the people who create, maintain, and support the corporate service culture.

All employees, but especially managers, need to have an appreciation and awareness of the company's history and culture, which includes the guiding principles on which the organization was founded, as well as the trials and tribulations, successes and accomplishments that the company has experienced over the years.

In this part, we recognize the value of consciously spreading a culture of service throughout the organization, including among new hires. This part also explores how you and your colleagues can provide your customers with more choices, which will give your customers more reasons to do business with your organization.

Nordstrom is a company whose managers constantly reinforce its history, its culture, its reason for being, and its unwavering dedication to *think like the customer.* This is the essence of a great customer-service company.

1

The Nordstrom Story

How a Century of Family Leadership Created a Culture of Entrepreneurship, Consensus, and Service

I know that the people who run the company are going to work as hard or harder than me. The same principles that were here before I got here will be in place after I retire. That's encouraging. I really like that.

(You can't teach culture. You have to live it. You have to experience it. You have to share it. You have to show it.)

—Brent Harris,
Nordstrom's national merchandise manager for shoes

Arriving at the lobby of the Nordstrom corporate offices, which is connected to the flagship store in downtown Seattle, a visitor is greeted first by the Nordstrom history and culture. On the walls adjacent to the elevators is a grainy, 100-year-old picture of founder John W. Nordstrom and his original partner, Carl F. Wallin, proudly standing outside their first tiny shoe store; and another shot, circa 1910, of the interior of the store, where mustachioed salesmen in rumpled suits are dwarfed by stacks and stacks of shoe boxes that are collected along the walls and piled high up to the ceiling.

New employees attend orientation on the fifth floor of this building, which contains the John W. Nordstrom room, where the company holds its annual shareholders meeting, customer events, staff meetings, and pep rallies. All around are pictures of stores, various generations of Nordstroms, and numerous other reminders of the rich Nordstrom heritage and culture. An appreciation of what Nordstrom is all about cannot be fully grasped without an understanding of the company's culture. That's why the importance and the value of the culture are emphasized from the moment new employees come to work for the company.

On one particular day, a dozen well-groomed and neatly dressed men and women are seated behind a horseshoe configuration of gray tables in a meeting room on the fifth floor of the corporate offices. They are a racially diverse group; most are under the age of 30, a couple are closer to 50. What they have in common is that they are all new employees, awaiting the start of the one-day employee orientation that kicks off their career at Nordstrom. In front of each one of them is a half-inch-thick blue folder. The one word on the cover is "Welcome."

On the inside, a separate sheet of paper contains these words:

> As we travel along the road of **life,** we encounter paths that lead to a great opportunity for **growth.** To recognize the doors that open to a bright **future** is the key. Once inside, we crave **support** from our colleagues. We know that the **health** of our relationships is paramount to our own **success,** and that the **joy** of sharing ideas leads to a **diversity** of options. Our reward is access to a **wealth** of knowledge that we would have otherwise overlooked. **Welcome** to Nordstrom. Our door is open.

Inside the packet are separate folders containing information on the company, employee guidelines, compensation program, safety program, and employee benefits. There is also a 5½-inch by 7½-inch card—the *Nordstrom Employee Handbook*. One side of the card says:

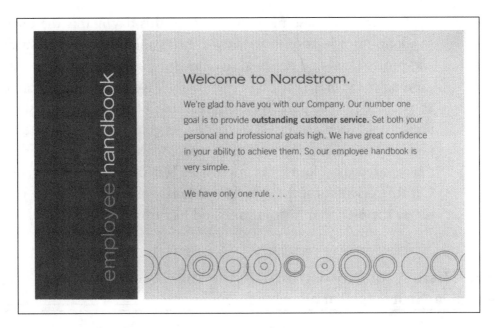

(Turning over the card)

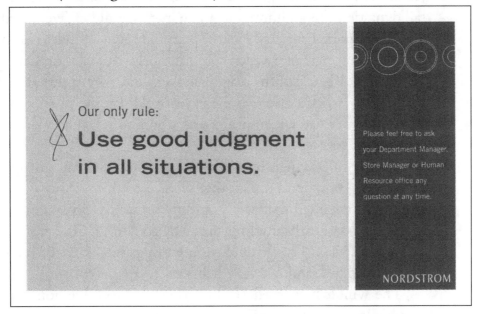

For some of these men and women, this day marks the birth of a long-term relationship that will bring them financial rewards and professional and personal fulfillment. For others, it is the beginning of the end. They will eventually leave Nordstrom because of what they will perceive as unreasonable demands, persistent pressure to <u>reach a ceaseless series of sales goals</u>, and relentless emphasis on providing the kind of all-encompassing customer service that has fed the Nordstrom mystique. But the future is for later. On this orientation day, these men and women are here to immerse themselves in that culture and its history.

The History of Nordstrom: After the Gold Rush, a Store Is Born

Johan W. Nordstrom, like the founders of most of America's retail dynasties, was an immigrant. The middle child of five, Nordstrom was born February 15, 1871, in the town of Lulea, in the northernmost part of Sweden, 60 miles below the Arctic Circle. His father, a blacksmith, wagon maker, and part-time farmer, passed away when Johan was eight years old. By the time he was 11, his mother had taken him out of school so he could work on the family farm.

His life in Sweden, by his own admission, was an unhappy one. As he got older, "my mother seemed to think I was a man, and often remarked that at my age my brother [10 years his senior] could do nearly anything and why couldn't I," he wrote. "I often cried when I had trouble doing things she expected me to do and couldn't, and felt very helpless."

The winter he turned 16, Johan decided to leave home and cast his lot in America. With 450 crowns (about $112) of his modest inheritance, given to him by his guardian, he bought a suit of clothes. "The first clothes I had ever had on my back that were not homespun and hand woven." His eventual destination was the Pacific Northwest of America, where thousands of Swedes thrived as fishermen, loggers, blacksmiths, shipwrights, and millwrights in a climate and landscape similar to their homeland. Others helped finish the transcontinental railroad. "Give me enough Swedes," proclaimed James J. Hill, the driving force behind the Great Northern Railroad, "and I'll build a railroad right through hell."

There were no railroads in northern Sweden, so Johan and two young friends began their odyssey with a two-day boat trip to Stockholm, followed by a three-day voyage across Sweden, through the Gota Canal, to Gothenburg, then on to Hull, in northeast England. The first train ride of Johan's life brought him to Liverpool, where he took steerage passage for the 10-day voyage to Ellis Island, New York. From there, Nordstrom and his friends, unable to speak a word of English, took a train to Stambaugh, Michigan, where he had a cousin and prospects for work.

When he arrived in Michigan, Nordstrom, with five dollars in his pocket, took a job hauling iron ore with a wheelbarrow, carting it about a hundred feet to a platform and dumping it into railroad cars. For the next five years, his strong back and fierce determination carried him westward through a series of hardscrabble manual labor jobs: logging in Michigan, digging coal in Iowa, mining gold and silver in Colorado, loading railroad ties and carting brick in Mendocino County, California, and Douglas fir trees in Washington state. By the summer of 1896, Nordstrom had saved enough money to buy 20 acres of bottom land for potato farming in the Swedish immigrant enclave of Arlington, Washington, about 50 miles north of Seattle.

Seattle: City of Opportunity _____

Seattle in the 1890s was "young, raw, and crude," wrote Roger Sale in *Seattle, Past to Present*. White settlers first reached the region in 1852. In 1860, a group of about 150 pioneers settled there. (By way of comparison, New York City in the 1850s already had paved streets and a store named R. H. Macy.) "They didn't come looking for paradise," said one wag. "They came for cheap real estate." From 1879 to 1890, population rocketed from 1,107 to 43,487, fueled by constant rumors that Seattle would be the terminus of the transcontinental railroad. The nascent city provided equal opportunity for God-fearing pioneers, entrepreneurial visionaries, scam artists, and ladies of the evening. The essence of the "Seattle Spirit" was "enlightened self-interest," wrote William C. Speidel, the city's iconoclastic historian, in his irreverent account, *Sons of the Profits*.

The mood was feverish. With Seattle about to be connected by rail via the Great Northern Railroad to the rest of North America, making money was on everyone's mind. A leading banker of that era, N. B. Coffman, described the 1890s as one "of adventure and wildcat speculation . . . such can never again be witnessed." Norman H. Clark wrote in *Washington: A Bicentennial History:* "There had been nothing like it in the American history since the opening of the Louisiana Territory—golden years where no personal ambition, however grandiose, seemed at all unreasonable, when it seemed that every venture might prosper and every family might share in the nobility of wealth because of the democracy of profit."

At breakfast, on Sunday morning, July 18, 1897, Johan Nordstrom picked up a copy of the *Seattle Post-Intelligencer* to see splashed across the front page, in huge capital letters, the magic word: "GOLD!" Coarse gold had been found in the fields of the Klondike, in Canada's Yukon Territory. Five thousand people greeted the steamer *Portland* when it arrived on July 17 at the Seattle waterfront with a much-ballyhooed cargo—"a ton of gold." Coupled with the arrival in San Francisco of the *Excelsior,* with another heavy cargo of gold, the news ignited the world.

Johan (who Anglicized his name to John) read the story "over and over again . . . discussing this big news," he recalled in his memoir. "Finally I slammed the paper down on the table and said, 'I'm going to Alaska!' " Nordstrom gathered his belongings and "what little money I had and by four o'clock that afternoon I was on the train bound for Seattle and a new adventure." Arriving at the Seattle waterfront early the following morning, he found a virtually endless line of people waiting to buy tickets for Alaska. When the coal freighter *Willamette* steamed out of Elliott Bay, Seattle, heading north for the Inland Passage, it was burdened with 1,200 men, 600 horses, 600 mules, and John Nordstrom. Because he had second-class passage, Nordstrom slept with the mules.

Reaching Port Valdez, Alaska, in Prince William Sound that summer, was merely the beginning of Nordstrom's thousand-mile adventure to his ultimate destination: Dawson, the frontier town in the heart of the gold fields. He battled cold, snow, rain, storms, and wind—mostly on foot, because his horse died along the way and had to be butchered for food. From Skagway, he walked over the frozen solid Klondike River into tiny Dawson, only a year old, but "as lively a little place as you'd ever see," he recalled. "There were many saloons, dance halls, and gambling houses, all waiting for the poor miner to spend his hard-earned gold."

For the next two years, Nordstrom struggled in the gold fields, taking a series of jobs to keep going. Finally, his luck changed: He struck gold. After Nordstrom staked his claim on the strike, another miner challenged it. The Canadian Gold Commission settled claim disputes but, unfortunately for Nordstrom, the man who made the competing claim was "a government man and a possible friend of the Gold Commissioner," Nordstrom wrote in his memoir. (Corruption was not unknown in the Yukon.) Nordstrom's friends advised him to sell his claim to the other man, rather than hold out and possibly wind up with nothing. After paying his legal expenses, Nordstrom ended up with $13,000 (more than $250,000 in today's dollars), which "looked like a lot of money to me, so I decided that I had had enough of Alaska and returned to Seattle," Nordstrom recalled. [The gold strike eventually netted the other man a reported $5 million.]

A booming Seattle was roaring into the twentieth century, fueled by the financial windfall of an unprecedented rush of new arrivals and the Klondike gold rush. "There was a swagger in its walk, a boldness in its vision," a historian wrote about Seattle. "Out here, on the edge of the continent, the great Pacific lapping at the front door, all things seemed possible."

In Seattle, John Nordstrom moved in with his sister. Sometime later, he renewed his acquaintance with Hilda Carlson, a Swedish girl he had taken out a few times before going to Alaska. Soon after, in May 1900, he married Hilda. They honeymooned in Sweden where they visited each other's homes, which were 24 miles apart.

"Looking around for some small business to get into," Nordstrom wrote in his privately published 1950 memoir, *The Immigrant in 1887,* he often visited an old Klondike pal, Carl F. Wallin, a shoemaker with a bushy walrus moustache, who had set up a little 10-foot-wide shoe repair shop on Fourth Avenue and Pike Street. Wallin suggested that he and Nordstrom form a partnership in a shoe store that would be established on the site of the repair shop. Nordstrom agreed, putting up $5,000; Wallin added $1,000. Some of the money was used to fix up the store, which was immediately expanded to 20 feet. With $3,500, they bought an inventory of shoes and opened their doors to customers in 1901. The store was named *Wallin & Nordstrom.*

Imagine Nordstrom, a 30-year-old man who had just purchased his first high-quality wool suit, ill fitting, no doubt, with fabric bunched up at the knees and elbows. He spoke only broken English and knew nothing about shoes or about selling. What he *did* know was that hard work and tenacity had always paid off for him. In his memoir, Nordstrom recalled the very first day of business:

> I had never fitted a pair of shoes or sold anything in my life, but I was depending on Mr. Wallin's meager knowledge of shoe salesmanship to help me out. Well, this opening day we had not had a customer by noon, so my partner went to lunch. He had not been gone but a few minutes when our first customer, a woman, came in for a pair of shoes she had seen in the window. I was nervous and could not find the style she had picked out in our stock. I was just about ready to give up when I decided to try on the pair from the window, the only pair we had of that style. I'll never know if it was the right size, but the customer bought them anyway.
>
> Opening day sales totaled $12.50.

The next day, Saturday, the store stayed open from eight o'clock in the morning until midnight; receipts were $47. By the end of that first summer, Saturday sales sometimes were as high as $100. "We both allowed ourselves a salary of $75 a month and got along fine on this amount," Nordstrom wrote.

What is important about the story of Wallin & Nordstrom's first sale is that John Nordstrom, without even realizing it, hit on one of the foundations of *The Nordstrom Way:* "Do whatever it takes to take care of the customer, and do whatever it takes to make sure the customer doesn't leave the store without buying something." More than a century later, the same principle still applies.

Wallin & Nordstrom steadily grew their business, periodically moving to larger spaces in downtown Seattle. Eventually, John's eldest sons, Everett W., born in 1903, and Elmer J., born a year later, began working in the store when each of them reached the age of 12, establishing a Nordstrom family tradition that has continued to this day across four generations. In the late 1920s, after gaining experience working for other retailers, Everett and Elmer bought out their father and Carl Wallin, and took ownership of the business, which comprised a couple of stores, employing about a dozen clerks. They soon changed the name of the store from Wallin & Nordstrom to "Nordstrom's." They would eventually settle on "Nordstrom." Years later, when friends asked John if he hadn't taken a big risk by putting virtually his entire net worth into the hands of his relatively inexperienced sons, he replied, "I only went through the sixth grade in grammar school in Sweden. My boys are college graduates. They must be a lot smarter than I ever was."

Elmer and Everett, who were later joined by their younger brother Lloyd, built Nordstrom's into the biggest independent shoe retailer in the United States. The company expanded into women's apparel in 1963, with the acquisition of a Seattle specialty shop called Best's Apparel, Inc., a fashionable downtown Seattle retailer, with a second store in downtown Portland, and renamed the company "Nordstrom Best." (John and Hilda's other children were daughters Esther and Mabel [who passed away in 1919], The daughters were not in the business.)

One of the reasons Nordstrom moved into apparel was to offer more opportunities for the third generation of Nordstroms, then in their thirties, including Everett's son, Bruce A.; Elmer's two sons, James F. and John N.; and John "Jack" McMillan, who was married to Lloyd's daughter, Loyal. All four were University of Washington graduates, with degrees in business. Like their fathers, the three younger Nordstroms began working in the store as children and continued to sell shoes throughout high school and college; McMillan also started working for the store while an undergraduate. Trained on the sales floor, the third generation was literally and figuratively "raised kneeling in front of the customer," said Bruce. In fact, they toiled for years in the stockroom before their fathers "ever allowed us near a foot."

In 1968, the brothers, whose net worth and only source of income was the corporation, wanted their estates to have a market value that could be readily established for the purpose of estate taxes. Their alternatives were to either sell the chain to the next generation or to an established retailer. Because the younger Nordstroms lacked the capital, the first option was not viable; but the second option was not only viable, it was preferable because it would make the brothers wealthy. Everett, Elmer, and Lloyd notified the third generation that they intended to sell the company, and soon three of the most prominent department store chains of that era—Associated Dry Goods, Dayton-Hudson, and Broadway-Hale Stores (the company later known as Carter Hawley Hale)—emerged as the prominent suitors. Jack McMillan recalled that as the offers began coming in, he and the young Nordstroms were forced to ask themselves whether they wanted to work for one of those three retail giants and, "the more we thought about it, we didn't."

Broadway-Hale made the most financially appealing offer: a million shares of Broadway-Hale stock at approximately $24 a share. The third generation, who would become significant Broadway-Hale stockholders, would continue to run the Nordstrom operation as a division of Broadway-Hale. For Jim Nordstrom, the most "sobering" experience came when he and his contemporaries were having lunch with Ed Carter, chairman of Broadway-Hale, who told the young Nordstroms how much he liked their stores and that they had done well through tough times in Seattle. He asked each of them how they were able to accomplish that. They explained that they used a decentralized management system. "John talked about the men's shoes business; Bruce about ladies' shoes; Jack and I talked about apparel," Jim Nordstrom recalled. "After we got all through [talking about the company's decentralized approach and decision-by-consensus style], Ed Carter said, 'You can't run a business like that.' I think we then all realized our job security was in jeopardy."

Before the senior Nordstroms entered into an agreement with Broadway-Hale, the younger Nordstroms came up with an alternative plan. They told their fathers that they could do a better job of running the company than any outside organization. Presenting Everett, Elmer, and Lloyd with a detailed business plan, they made the case that they could successfully steer the business. Part of their plan entailed paying for the transaction by issuing stock and taking the company public, which would be an extraordinary move for a firm that prided itself on its low profile and the fact that it had financed expansion solely out of earnings.

"We asked them to entrust their fortune to us," said Bruce. They had their doubts. "They looked at us and they weren't thrilled with what they saw," Jim recollected. "So, the idea of [ensuring their] security and selling it to another company appealed to them." The brothers believed the main reason they succeeded was their ability to work together as a cohesive unit. They didn't know if the younger generation, who had always gotten along (but had not had the opportunity to work as a group) could duplicate that solidarity. "And we didn't want to see them break up into feuding factions trying to," recalled Elmer.

Despite their misgivings, the brothers, who were encouraged by the four boys' ability to organize themselves, accepted their proposal. "We were shocked," said Jim Nordstrom. "We thought they would take the money."

The pro forma proposal put together by the third generation estimated that Nordstrom would reach $100 million in sales by 1980. As it turned out, they underestimated that number by almost $400 million.

In May 1970, Bruce, then 37; John, 34; Jim, 31; and Jack McMillan, 39, assumed operating management. The following year, the three Nordstroms became co-presidents and directors, and drew the same salary. Elmer, Everett, and Lloyd became co-chairmen of the board, "offering encouragement and resisting the temptation to give advice," wrote Elmer. As the torch was passed, the older brothers emphasized the need for constant diligence, "because from our experience during the war years, we saw how easily a business could fall apart from neglect." They gave the boys a long list of potential excuses—including the weather, the economy, and the new shopping center down the block. "We told them they might as well give us their excuses by the number, because they didn't mean a thing. If business was bad, there was nowhere to put the blame but upon themselves."

Like their predecessors, the third generation emulated the decision-by-consensus approach, and it worked; whatever private disagreements they had were never known by anyone outside their inner circle.

In May 1978, Nordstrom, which some were calling the "Bloomingdale's of the West," expanded into California, with a 124,000 sq. ft., three-level store at the South Coast Plaza shopping center in Costa Mesa. This store boasted the biggest shoe department in the state of California—10,000 sq. ft. for women's shoes, 3,000 for men's, and 2,500 for children's. Although the Nordstrom name was barely known, the store became an instant success, and quickly became the biggest volume store in the chain.

The third generation grew the company to 61 full-line stores in Washington, Alaska, Oregon, California, Utah, Texas, Minnesota, Indiana, Illinois, Pennsylvania, Virginia, Maryland, New Jersey, and New York; twenty clearance and off-price stores; a Faconnable men's wear boutique in New York City, and leased shoe departments in 12 department stores in Hawaii and Guam—with total sales of $4.1 billion and a reputation as America's Number One customer service company. In 1995, Nordstrom's third generation of leaders all stepped down as co-chairman, but continued serving on the board of directors and as members of the board's executive committee.

In 2000, after several difficult years for the company, Bruce's oldest son, Blake Nordstrom, became president, becoming the first fourth-generation Nordstrom to lead the company.

Clearly, the continuity of family management is one of the most important reasons for Nordstrom's success. The active presence and involvement of family members is the guarantee that Nordstrom will remain Nordstrom; without them, it would be a different company. The Nordstroms have been involved and instrumental in every aspect of the company. (At store openings, the family meets with every new hire.)

"It's so powerful when they come around to talk to our people and remind them that our company is only as good as they are today and every day," said Len Kuntz, executive vice president and regional manager of the Washington/Alaska region. Decades earlier, Elmer, Lloyd, and Everett used to put on annual summer picnics for employees, their wives, and children at the family's summer place on Hood Canal on Washington State's Olympic Peninsula, and Christmas dinner dance parties at Seattle's stately Olympic Hotel.

The Nordstrom Family: Leading by Example

Within the company and the consuming public, the Nordstroms are approachable and accessible. All of them answer their own phones—and return calls; this has been true through four generations. Tom Peters used to mention this at his seminars, and during a lunch break at one of those seminars, a man decided to test this claim—unbeknownst to Peters. After the lunch break, the man announced to the audience that he had, in fact, just called Bruce Nordstrom. Bruce wasn't in his office but the call was patched through to him on the sales floor, and they had a 15-minute conversation.

Peters, a big fan of the company, once wrote about a man who wrote a letter describing his difficulty in getting a suit that he had purchased at Nordstrom to fit—despite several visits for alterations. When John N. Nordstrom got the letter, he sent over a new suit to the customer's office, along with a Nordstrom tailor to make sure the jacket and pants were perfect. When alterations were completed, the suit was delivered at no charge.

A woman who worked at Nordstrom in the 1980s, told Robert Spector a story about Bruce Nordstrom walking through her department one day. Bruce spotted a can of pop on the counter. He picked up the can, deposited it in a wastebasket, and continued on his way. (He didn't ask who was responsible for the can being on the counter and he didn't order an employee to take it away. He just did it himself.) This woman, who went on to run several of her own successful businesses, never forgot the day that she saw the chairman of the company set an example for her— without his even uttering a word.

Despite their success, the Nordstroms continue to insist on projecting a public image of disarming, small-town modesty that might strike an observer as disingenuous. They say that there is nothing special or magical or difficult about what they do and that the system is embarrassingly simple. "We outservice, not outsmart," is a typical Nordstromism. They rarely talk about themselves. "We can't afford to boast. If we did, we might start to believe our own stories, get big heads, and stop trying," Jim Nordstrom once said. When Bruce was selected as *Footwear News* magazine's Man of the Year, he politely declined the award and refused to be interviewed for the article.

"It's not about us," said Bruce's son, Blake, who described his role and that of his family members as "stewards of the business and the culture. We are here to help everyone achieve his or her goals. Companies that have a strong culture have an asset—a point of difference. We try to create an atmosphere where people feel valued, trusted and respected, and empowered, where they have a proprietary feeling and an entrepreneurial spirit. The magic occurs when all these things come together."

A Seattle journalist once compared the Nordstrom family to Mount Rainier. "As the mountain symbolizes the beauty and splendor of the Northwest," wrote Fred Moody in *Seattle Weekly,* "so the Nordstrom name has come to epitomize a certain Northwestness of character, a set of drives and values that we regard as being unique to our corner of the country."

With few exceptions, the great stores of America are no longer controlled or operated by the descendants of the clever merchants who created the business and knew what the customer wanted. It's not that professional managers can't brilliantly run the Macy's, Saks, and Neiman Marcuses of the world; it's just that in an era when top retail executives change department stores as fast as free agents switch baseball teams, continuity is measured by quarterly earnings, not generations. The connection to the founder's original vision usually vanishes by the second generation.

While tradition and leadership continuity is important, the Nordstrom family is not insulated from non–Nordstrom thinking. The majority of the board of directors is comprised of outside advisors with no vested interest in the company, and the management team is a mix of nonfamily and family members.

Alfred E. Osborne Jr., a long-time Nordstrom director and professor of business economics at UCLA, told Robert Spector that Nordstrom's entrepreneurial, yet consensus-seeking approach to business has distinct advantages over the typical hierarchical business model ". . . because the world is moving to greater participation, more shared decisions, more decisions at the point of service. Workers at all levels of the organization are empowered by both technology and information, all of which means more collaboration, all of which means shrinking hierarchies. Which means that the old-fashioned Nordstrom approach to management may be what the twenty-first century is all about and is what will be increasingly adopted by a variety of organizations."

The people attending the employee orientation that started this chapter, like all other Nordstrom employees, will become steeped in the culture. They will learn the values that the company supports and the atmosphere it tries to create where everyone is in a position to succeed. All of that comes from the top and works its way throughout every part of the organization. What they learn in their careers can be found in the rest of this book.

EXERCISE

What Is Our Company's History?

Most companies and organizations have an interesting history. After all, they were created for specific reasons—filling a void in the market, coming up with a new idea, a new product, and so on.

(Appoint an employee to be the official or unofficial company historian. That person will assemble relevant documents, newspaper articles, corporate reports, and so on, and interview the founders or other key executives to get a flavor of the history and, ultimately, the culture.)

Ask the following questions:

- Who founded this company?
- Why was the company founded?
- What kind of challenges did the founder face?
- Was there a time when it looked like the company was headed for failure?
- How was the company able to overcome adversity and survive?
- Has the company appreciably changed its business over the years?
- How has the company responded to the market?

(Continued)

(Continued)

- Once the information is assembled, distribute it to all members of your organization.

- Assign a committee of employees to come up with a Jeopardy-like program that covers your company history.

- Organize an assembly of employees who have studied the material and play the Jeopardy game. This can be fun and educational. Don't forget to include prizes.
  — EXTERNAL REWARDS —

2

Spreading the Service Culture

Publicly Celebrate Your Heroes; Promote from Within

There is nothing so nice as doing good by stealth and being found out by accident.

—Charles Lamb,
English essayist

Storytelling and folklore play a critical role in spreading Nordstrom's values and priorities around the company. In fact, stories of customer service and teamwork above-and-beyond the call of duty have their own word at Nordstrom: "heroics." Heroics serve as ready reminders of the level of service to which all employees should aspire. They also represent an ideal way to pass on a company's (any company's) cultural values.

Nordstrom "Heroics"

Employees who witness a colleague giving customer service above and beyond the call of duty are encouraged to write up a description of what they saw and submit it to their manager. Stories of heroics are regularly shared among salespeople. Frequent subjects of the heroics are selected as Customer Service All-Stars with their pictures mounted in the customer service area in the store where they work. The purpose of heroics is to give Nordstrom people a standard to aspire to—and even to surpass. The cumulative effect of this continual reinforcement at (Nordstrom is that the frontline workers soon see that the people who run their company single out, honor, and reward outstanding acts of customer service.) And those workers quickly learn that the way to advance in the company is to give great customer service. "If you see a great example, you're going to imitate that," said Len Kuntz, executive vice president of the Washington/Alaska region.

There are many great examples of heroics. For example, there is the story of a customer who fell in love with a pair of burgundy, pleated Donna Karan slacks that had just gone on sale at the Nordstrom store in downtown Seattle. But the store was out of her size, and the salesperson was unable to track down a pair at the five other Nordstrom stores in the Seattle area. Aware that the same slacks were available across the street at a competitor, the salesperson secured some petty cash from her department manager, marched across the street to a competing retailer, where she bought the slacks (at full price), returned to Nordstrom and then sold them to the customer for the marked-down Nordstrom price. Obviously, Nordstrom didn't make money on that sale, but it was an investment in promoting the loyalty of an appreciative customer, who thought of Nordstrom for her next purchase.

A man who was involved in sales for a scientific supply company wrote the store manager of the Nordstrom store at the Old Orchard Shopping Center in Skokie, Illinois, about a great customer service experience that he wanted to share. The man had an unusual size, 6½ EE, and had been having major problems finding a pair of black wingtip shoes in downtown Chicago, where he lived. At a specialty shoe store downtown near his home, the salesman happily sold him a pair of Florsheim wing tips for $97 and assured the customer that the shoes were the right size. The customer had tried them on hurriedly and bought them. But when he put them on the following day, he immediately sensed that they were not feeling right—and no wonder; they were actually size 7!

"I returned them and informed the store of the mistake and asked if I could get a wingtip in my size," the customer later recalled. "The sales clerk said they didn't stock my size and it would be a special order at an additional cost. I said I don't have the time to wait and would like to return them for a refund on my credit card. The store manager refused the refund and gave me store credit instead. I asked him how could I get store credit if they don't have a shoe in my size? What would I do, buy $97 in socks? So I left angry."

After two days of shopping in countless shoe stores, the man came to the unhappy realization that no one in the city of Chicago carried his size—and if they did it would take two weeks to special order the shoes.

Finally, a friend told him about Nordstrom's extensive shoe department, so he drove out to suburban Skokie, where salesman Rich Komie waited on him. Komie measured the man's feet and came back from the stockroom with six pairs of black wingtips that fit perfectly, and fully explained the benefits of each type.

"I was elated!," wrote the customer, who told Rich Komie about the crummy treatment he had received at a competitor's store in Chicago. When he heard the story, Komie didn't just sympathize with the customer, no, he called the competitor's store and asked them to refund the customer's money. Imagine getting a call from Nordstrom questioning you on your customer service? What else could the salesman from the other store do but give the customer a full refund? The customer ended up buying two pairs of shoes that day from Rich Komie and Nordstrom. "I have never had a more pleasurable experience buying shoes in my life," the customer concluded in a letter to Nordstrom. "Rich even put me in contact with the Nordstrom's tailor for a suit that needed a few adjustments! It didn't end there, Rich even sent me a thank-you card!" After that experience, the man concluded, "I now tell this story to all my new manufacturers reps that I train and emphasize how total customer satisfaction means not just THE SALE but REPEAT SALES!!"

Nordstrom has never run an advertisement boasting about its customer service. Nordstrom has never issued a press release about a great act of customer service performed by one of their employees. Everything you've heard or read about Nordstrom's customer service has been through word-of-mouth.

And some of the best heroics have nothing to do with making a sale.

One of my favorites is the story of the customer who made a last-minute shopping stop at the Nordstrom store in downtown before heading out to Seattle-Tacoma International Airport to catch a flight. After the customer left the store, her Nordstrom salesperson discovered the customer's airplane ticket on the counter. The saleswoman called a representative of the airline and asked if they could write the customer another ticket at the airport. Have you ever lost an airplane ticket? Of course the airline said they couldn't reticket the customer. They have rules against that sort of thing. What did the Nordstrom saleswoman do? She jumped into action. She took some money from petty cash, hailed a taxi cab, which took her to the Seattle-Tacoma International Airport, where she was able to page the customer and hand her the ticket. That was one appreciative customer. And it's important to remember that the saleswoman, who worked on commission, took at least an hour-and-a-half out of her day to do a good deed.

On a business trip to Seattle, Dr. Charlene Smith from Athens, Ohio, was shopping in Nordstrom in downtown Seattle. Dr. Smith had accidentally left her 14-karat gold necklace behind in the fitting room as she hurried off to a convention banquet at a nearby hotel. When Connie Corcoran, her salesperson, discovered the necklace, she immediately phoned the hotel trying to locate Dr. Smith.

At first, the hotel staff was reluctant to help in the search for Dr. Smith because she wasn't a registered guest. But Connie insisted they check the banquet roster and find her customer. Eventually the hotel employee found Dr. Smith at her banquet table and surprised her saying that "a woman from Nordstrom was on the phone" to inform her she had left "something valuable" in the store.

Though Charlene Smith had been unaware the necklace was missing, she knew immediately who would be on the phone and why. When Connie arrived in the hotel lobby with the necklace a few minutes later, Dr. Smith ran up and hugged her, thanking her for what she'd done. (How many people do you think Dr. Smith told that story to?)

Several more "heroics" are cited throughout this book as well as in the appendix in the back of the book.

Great customer service is in the details; in simple human kindness.

After Robert Spector gave a speech in Indianapolis to a convention of tour operators, a woman came up to him and said, "I have a Nordstrom story for you, but it's too complicated to tell it to you here." Robert asked her to send him an e-mail, which, thankfully, she did.

Here is her letter:

Last Fall, I accompanied my 33-year-old sister, Cindi, to Seattle where she was to undergo a bone marrow transplant for leukemia. If you've ever seen anyone after they've gone through one of these things, you would think they had been in a concentration camp. Skinny, no hair—not even eyebrows, pale and sickly looking. My sister had an especially hard time and ended up in a wheelchair for a few weeks due to muscle weakness.

After she was discharged from the Fred Hutchinson Cancer Institute, we stayed in Seattle for a few months to keep a constant watch on her progress. At one point, the doctor cleared Cindi to take a few "road trips" to get out of the apartment. Her favorite thing to do was go shopping, so we hauled the wheelchair and my sister to downtown Seattle and ended up in Nordstrom's. Since we are from the East Coast, we had heard of the reputation of Nordstrom's customer service but never actually visited a store. [This story occurred before Nordstrom opened stores on the East Coast in the late 1980s.]

Picture me wheeling around my sister, pale and sickly looking. (I forgot to mention that my sister was a model and always took pride in her appearance.) Well, most people avoided us because she looked awful! We were going through the cosmetics area of Nordstrom's when a woman from the Estée Lauder counter stepped out in front of us and asked if she could put some make up on my sister! God love her, I don't know her name, but for a half hour, my sister felt like a million bucks. This cosmetics saleswoman knew she wouldn't make a sale because my sister looked like she was about to die, but she knew she could make a difference in my sister's last days.

My sister died shortly thereafter, but I will always remember the woman who made her feel like a beautiful human being—knowing she wouldn't make a sale, but she made a difference.

Now that's a heroic; that's a story produced in a company that stands for something.

Using Experienced "Nordies" to Spread the Culture _____

Because Nordstrom considers its culture the key element separating it from the competition, when the company expands to other regions, it relies on experienced "Nordies" to transfer to these new markets, to bring the culture with them and to teach and inspire new employees in customer service the Nordstrom way.

Betsy Sanders, the former Nordstrom executive (and former board member of Wal-Mart Stores, Inc.), who in the late 1970s was put in charge of Nordstrom's move to California, the company's first expansion outside of the Pacific Northwest, recalled that California was "fraught with challenge but it was exciting. There was no matrix, no plan, no instruction, which had always been how Nordstrom worked. Except this was on a bigger scale than we normally did it. We invented this region as we went along." One of Sanders's first orders of business was to recruit people to work in the store. "No one had been hired with the exception of the shoe buyer. At first, we were told that we could not find anyone in Southern California to give the kind of service that we had developed a reputation for. And if we did, it wouldn't matter because we would find no customers interested in us. We were virtually unknown in Southern California. People would stand in the middle of the mall and look down toward our end and say, 'What's a Nordstein?' I heard that more than once. The only people who had heard of us were those who had lived in the Northwest, and they were crazy about the fact that we were coming."

To attract new employees, Nordstrom ran a clever newspaper advertisement with the headline, "Wanted: People Power," accompanied by copy that described the attributes that Nordstrom was looking for. "It didn't say what we were. It didn't say what jobs were available," said Sanders. "On the strength of that ad, we had over 1,500 applicants. The personnel manager, the customer service manager, customer credit manager, and myself interviewed all 1,500; again, many of them had never heard of Nordstrom, but they loved what the ad called for." In keeping with the Nordstrom policy of hiring from within, all the new buyers and department managers for the California store were company veterans.

"The customers liked us, but our competitors waited for us to send everybody back to Seattle," said Sanders. "They presumed we just brought in [customer service experts] for the opening and that it would then be back to business as usual. Well, it never turned into business as usual. Eventually, competitors began telling employees in their training classes that they were going to have to start smiling and being nice to the customer because Nordstrom was coming and that's how Nordstrom salespeople act. They never got the point: It wasn't an act."

A decade later, when Nordstrom opened its first East Coast store in Tysons Corner, Virginia, a suburb of Washington, D.C., about 90 experienced Nordstrom department managers moved to Virginia from California, Washington, Oregon, Utah, and Alaska, and more than 300 veteran Nordstrom salespeople volunteered to relocate at their own expense. They were motivated by opportunities to move ahead in the company.

"It was exciting because we knew we were involved in something from the ground up," said Len Kuntz, one of those pioneers, who transferred to Tysons Corner as a men's wear buyer (and who is today executive vice president/regional manager of the Washington/Alaska region). "Having only one store in the region at that time, the buyers and merchandise managers were on the floor all the time, interacting with the salespeople and the customers and getting involved in the community. That helped nail down our philosophies a lot quicker than anything else and gave the store a distinct personality." Still, Kuntz and others had a lot of convincing to do when recruiting new salespeople. "For a long time, a lot of people who started with us thought of us as just another department store. Their image of a department store was a place where you hang out for a while before you get a 'real' job. They thought of it in terms of being a clerk, as opposed to a salesperson involved in the business. They were used to just standing by a register and ringing up stuff when the customer brought it to them. We had a little bit of turnover there."

In 1990, when Bob Middlemas, executive vice president and Midwest regional manager, was charged with putting together a team "to do the very best job in indoctrinating the Nordstrom culture in the Midwest region. I went to every region of the company and talked to people who had sent me letters of interest in being part of the new Chicago team. I met with all those people. From those meetings, I was able to pick my core team, which consisted of about 20 people. Those folks hired people in different levels of management in our division. We came out with 100 seasoned Nordstrom employees; all of us worked in about 4,000 sq. ft. of temporary office space, so we became very close."

At employee orientation, Middlemas and some of the other veteran Nordies spoke to new hires about how the company operates. More dramatically, department managers got up and told their stories about how they started with the company. "It wasn't just their words," Middlemas recalled. "These people were so proud of our company and their accomplishments and so appreciative of a company that allowed them to prosper. They would start to cry; their eyes would well up. In the audience, there were people crying along with them, who were really touched by this." This is how a culture of excellence spreads!

Promoting from Within

When Nordstrom expanded into women's apparel in 1963, they hired a well-regarded women's apparel retail specialist for their new operation, and at least at first, "We marveled at him. He was just what we thought a dress buyer ought to be," Bruce Nordstrom told *Forbes* magazine in 1978. "But one day we were having a meeting to plan our normal sales contest and we said, 'All right, the winners get steak and the losers get beans.' Well, I was walking out behind this guy and he turned to someone and said, 'This is the most sophomoric thing I've ever heard.' I guess it was, but he was at the bottom of all our performance lists. He's a substantial guy in the industry, but he was not for us."

(From then on, Nordstrom instituted a policy of never hiring managers from outside companies.) The danger of hiring and promoting from within is that it can lead to uniform thinking. Nordstrom, however, believes that only people who have started at the bottom and worked their way up through the system can have a full appreciation of the company's unique culture.

In the 1960s, as Nordstrom began its ambitious expansion, the company created a fast career track for up-and-coming employees. Some became buyers in their early twenties; one store manager was just 23; one shoe buyer was a mere 20. Nordstrom continues to find ways to attract good people and keep them motivated with opportunities to ascend the corporate ladder. "With our decentralized system, each division has a life of its own," said Bruce Nordstrom. "If people are carrying out their missions and we feel good about the way they are developing, we will have ourselves new regional managers and buyers as we go into new regions." Leaders with a deep understanding of the Nordstrom culture, and who really live the values, can't be bought from a competitor for a high salary. They must be grown from within.

"The empowered, decentralized, entrepreneurial spirit of this company has blossomed as the company has grown," said Erik Nordstrom. "I don't think it would have blossomed if we didn't grow. People wouldn't have seen the opportunities and would not have stayed. There are lots of examples of people who have had great careers with this company. They started on the selling floor and grew with the company. They are the ones who are responsible for our reputation."

EXERCISE

Tell the Story of Your Company's Heroes

As we have seen, storytelling is an essential way for Nordstrom to promote and sustain its culture. There are great stories in your organization. Your assignment is to find them and spread the word about them:

- Ask employees to submit great stories of customer service— *heroics.*

- These can be stories concerning both internal and external customers.

- Ask employees to submit great stories of *teamwork* among employees.

- Distribute these stories.

(Continued)

(Continued)

- Offer prizes for the best stories.
- Find ways to encourage, honor, and reward outstanding acts of customer service.

EXERCISE

What Do We Stand For?

In this activity, brainstorm on the qualities that make your organization unique. You will be able to form the foundation for illustrating and spreading the word on your culture.

- We don't mean creating a mission statement. Mission statements are generally the products of committees, and sound that way.
- Assemble a group of people from all parts of your organization. Give everyone a pad and pen. Give yourself 10 minutes to answer these questions:

Question 1: What do we stand for?

Question 2: What are the qualities that make our organization unique?

Question 3: How do we see ourselves?

Question 4: How do our competitors see us?

Question 5: How do our customers see us?

Question 6: How do our suppliers see us?

(Continued)

(Continued)

- Put together a master list of all your answers.

- Discuss the results.

- Edit the results down to a few workable sentences that encapsulate what the company stands for.

- Distribute that list to all members of your organization.

- Include the list in your employee handbook.

- Encourage and reward employees who live up to those qualities.

3

Line Up and Cheer for Your Customer

Create an Inviting Place to Do Business

*Be not forgetful to entertain strangers,
For thereby some have entertained angels unawares.*

—Hebrews 13:2

I t is the day women across the city have been waiting for," gushed the beautifully coifed and tailored Houston TV news anchorwoman. "Friday marks the opening of Houston's first Nordstrom store at the Galleria Mall."

Cut to an attractive 30-something African American woman: "We are so glad they finally came to Houston. It's going to be fabulous. The store is so great. The customer service is fabulous. We look forward to having Nordstrom in Houston."

The scene shifts to a local TV newscast, a few months later; this one in Austin, Texas.

"It's the moment Austin shoppers have been waiting for," said the bespectacled anchorman, a slight smile creasing his face. "It was a madhouse today at Barton Creek Mall."

Cut to a 40-something blonde shopper: "There's no place else I would rather be. I've been countin' this down for about six months," she drawls. "We're going to be in there all day. I don't plan on leaving the store."

Cut to a shot of thousands of pumped up women (and a smattering of men) outside the new Nordstrom store, waiting patiently (some impatiently) for the doors to open for the first time, shouting "Nordstrom! Nordstrom! Nordstrom!" as if they were cheering for the University of Texas Longhorns football team.

Meanwhile at the entrance to the store, a big brown rolldown door momentarily separates the customers from the sales staff. Excitement is building on both sides of the 30-foot-wide divider. It's hard to tell who is more eager—the shoppers or the salespeople. Finally, at precisely 9:30 A.M., the door slowly inches upward like a giant garage door. Hyperkinetic shoppers in front of the throng hardly hesitate to wait for the divider to raise up all the way. They duck underneath and begin dashing into the store in a scene reminiscent of the running of the bulls at Pamplona. Some are dancing, some are skipping, some with feet barely touching the marble floor beneath them—they are being high-fived by beaming Nordstrom employees, who have lined up at the entrance to applaud and cheer the new shoppers—a longstanding company tradition.)

"Fabulous styles, wonderful service. I've become a part of it in California and I just can't quit," enthuses an ecstatic Vivian Picow, a long-time customer, who proudly holds up a T-shirt that features a picture of her holding her car license plate that is in a holder that proclaims: "I'd rather be shopping at Nordstrom." One of the highlights for her on that day was when she got Blake, Pete, and Erik Nordstrom to autograph her T-shirt. This scene is repeated in Charlotte, Richmond, Boca Raton, Las Vegas; even Michigan Avenue in Chicago, which is one of the world's greatest retail venues. There is nothing quite like the opening of a new Nordstrom store to quicken the pulse—and open the purse—of serious shoppers. This, you might say, is the "Nordstrom Effect"—the way you set the stage for creating an inviting place for your customers.

Having opened nearly 100 stores in every corner of the United States, Nordstrom has perfected an opening day plan of attack as precise as the invasion of Normandy on D-Day.

Key to the Nordstrom expansion strategy is to open stores in new markets "with all guns blazing," said chairman Bruce Nordstrom. "I think we get off to a running start better than anybody.

We say, 'let's be beautiful, let's be great, let's have a beautiful opening party, and donate lots of money to local charity.' [Usually through a fashion show/benefit before the store officially opens.] We haven't made a cent yet, but we're going to do those things first."

What's Inside

What's inside the store—the residential feeling, layout, design, lighting, seating, wide aisles, larger fitting rooms, display fixtures, amenities, and, of course, the merchandise—is an essential facet of customer service the Nordstrom way.

With convenience and openness the trademarks of its store design, Nordstrom wants to make it as easy as possible for customers to circulate and shop throughout the entire store, and for salespeople to help them do just that.

"When customers first come into the store, we've got about 15 seconds to get them excited about it," said retired co-chairman John N. Nordstrom, who is considered something of a student of store design and customer reaction. "First, are they able to meander through the store without impediments, such as narrow aisles? When they're walking down an aisle, and another customer is coming the other way, do they have enough room to pass? If the answer is 'no,' all of a sudden they're distracted. Instead of looking at the nice sweater, they've got a stroller banging them in the ankles. When they think about our store, they don't think of jostling and banging, they think of it as a pleasant experience. What's that worth?"

Store layouts typically resemble a wheel. The "hub" of the wheel is the escalator well; the spokes are the marbled aisles that lead directly back to each of the 30 or so departments. The subtleties and details create a shopping experience that is easy, convenient, and pleasurable. Most department stores in suburban malls have just one elevator; Nordstrom has two elevators in its three-level stores. (In Nordstrom's two-level stores, there is one elevator, but that one elevator is larger than elevators found in other department stores.) The waiting areas around elevators are extra wide to make it easy for customers to navigate with baby strollers or in wheelchairs, and the elevators themselves are larger than average, making it easier to load and unload those strollers and wheelchairs. Escalators are 42 inches wide—compared with the 36-inch-wide escalators found in most other department stores—allowing spouses or children to ride side-by-side. Unobstructed sight lines enable the customers riding on the escalators to quickly scrutinize the full spectrum of the selling floor. The aisles give shoppers the freedom to circle the store and to plunge into the center of each individual department. (Nordstrom believes that if you can lure customers to the perimeter back walls of the store, they are more apt to make a purchase.) "If someone wants to walk all the way around the store, they're not fighting through traffic, even on the busiest day. That's important because, sometimes, that's the only time we get that customer in the store," said John N. Nordstrom.

Unlike large retailers who close off their departments with walls or dividers, Nordstrom features departments that are freestanding. These departments are defined by lighted curtains, secondary aisles, upholstered lounge seating, custom-designed hardwood, bronze, and glass showcases; and furnishings and display fixtures that are built low, so as not to obscure shoppers' views of other departments, or salespeople's views of customers. Spaces in virtually every department are made warm and comfortable by the furnishings, as well as plants, plush carpeting, lighting, wainscoting, and artwork. The merchandise is presented in succinct, compelling visual displays that Nordstrom describes as "aspirational"—that is, merchandise that customers aspire to buy. The displays change regularly to maintain interest among frequent shoppers.

Secondary aisles that run through the back of the departments are about 10 feet from the back wall. Along the back walls, the merchandise is highlighted and romanced, like artwork in a gallery, by spot lighting and warm wall coverings instead of paint.

"We've spent all this money on the store. Let's make every square foot as important as we can rather than just the front end of the store," said John N. Nordstrom. "In the old days, we used to push everything toward the front; the back of the store was only sale stuff. That's nuts. We can be more efficient than that."

At the end of extended aisles, Nordstrom prefers to situate destination areas such as a home department, restaurant, dressing room, or lounge, rather than run the aisle into a wall. "When there's nothing down at the other end, it's jarring to the customer," added John N. Nordstrom. "But if there's something down there, they want to see what it is."

With its heritage as a shoe store, Nordstrom's footwear departments (most stores have four or five separate departments) are its showplaces. As a convenience, women's shoes are always located near the most prominent store entrance. Because shoes are the most important customer draw (after all, most people have a hard time finding a pair that fits), the company devotes about three times more space to its women's shoe department than its competitors and fills that space with more inventory than any other store offers. As an extreme example, The Mall of America store in Minneapolis stocks over 125,000 different sizes, styles, and colors; a more typical suburban store will carry 70,000 pairs.

Let's Get Comfortable

At newer Nordstrom stores, half the footwear inventory in each department is stocked directly behind that department, which makes a sale easier and less time-consuming for both the salesperson and the customer. (The other half of the footwear inventory is stocked in mezzanines, which are directly above the shoe stock, adjacent to the sales floor.) With so much of the stockroom merchandise nearby, salespeople don't have to hustle up and down stairs all day; they can get in and out of the shoe stockroom in a couple of minutes.

Because Nordstrom carries so many shoes, and because most feet are tough to fit, Nordstrom knows that customers are going to be in the footwear department for a while, so they make sure the customers are comfortable. Seating is sturdy enough to withstand the constant wear that's a fact of life in a bustling shoe department. While most other retailers fill their shoe departments with a line of half a dozen or so straight-back chairs, Nordstrom creates a homey parlor or lounge feeling with plushy upholstered sofas and as many as 50 to 75 upholstered chairs. These chairs are custom-made because the typical department store chair is not durable, or tall enough to meet Nordstrom specifications. Chair legs and armrests are made a bit taller than average, and the seating is firmer, which makes it easier for a person to stand up. Consequently, customers need only focus on how the shoe feels; they have no difficulty getting up out of the chair. Nordstrom doesn't want the customer to have to think about getting in and out of that chair; Nordstrom wants the customer to think only about those shoes—and perhaps buying another pair or two.

Each day, each footwear department designates a particular shoe style as the hot "item of the day," giving it greater emphasis among the salesforce. Inventories of the item of the day are stockpiled just inside the stockroom door so that they are readily available to salespeople, who sometimes receive extra bonuses for selling those featured items.

Not surprisingly, customers frequently comment on how comfortable the seating is throughout the store; husbands and boyfriends can be found sitting restfully, waiting for their ladies, rather than hurrying them out of the store. Nordstrom knows that customers will stay a little longer and try on one more shoe if they—and their gentlemen—are comfortable.

A Seattle writer named J. Glenn Evans, who penned this poem, entitled "A Place to Rest,"* summed up Nordstrom's consideration for customer comfort:

> I followed my wife
> While she shopped
> From store to store
> she went
>
> I the great man
> was spent
> The flesh pulled on my bones
> like two bags of cement
>
> At last I found a chair
> Heaven only
> could have been more fair
>
> Of all the stores
> Nordstrom was best
> They gave a husband
> a place to rest.

*Used with permission of the author.

When you have your customers writing love poems to you, you know you are doing a pretty good job.

One of the Nordstrom touches that keeps shoppers in the store is the retailer's live piano player, which has long been a Nordstrom signature that engages a customer's senses, and creates the ambiance of an inviting place. Usually located by the escalator, the Nordstrom piano has become something of a cultural icon. Condoleeza Rice, the Secretary of State for President George W. Bush (and a trained classical pianist) once joked that her ability was just good enough to get her a job playing at Nordstrom. In the novel, *Sleeping with Schubert* by Bonnie Marson, the heroine (a neophyte musician) suddenly channels the classical composer when she spontaneously begins to play a piano at a Nordstrom store, setting off a series of events that eventually leads to her giving a recital at Lincoln Center in New York (New York: Random House, 2004).

Leonard Lauder, retired chairman and chief executive officer of Estée Lauder Cos., once commented that, "A Nordstrom piano doesn't take up much room. It's a small idea, but it's a genius idea."

Nordstrom's large, carpeted dressing rooms, fitting rooms, and customer lounges are furnished with upholstered chairs and/or sofas. Fitting rooms in the more fashionable ready-to-wear departments include tables, table lamps, and telephones. Particular attention is given to the lighting of the mirrors in the dressing rooms. Nordstrom uses a combination of incandescent and fluorescent lights so that the customer can see the actual colors of the item being purchased. Reducing the use of incandescent lighting had the added benefit of keeping down the temperature in the dressing rooms. Nordstrom also adjusts the coolness of the dressing rooms with a dedicated thermostat that is separate from the thermostats that control the temperature on the sales floor and in the adjoining rooms. Although independent thermostats add to Nordstrom's costs, they also add to the customers' comfort. When a customer is sequestered in a small, hot, and stuffy room, trying clothes on and then taking them off, that customer will invariably want to get through the experience as quickly as possible. Nordstrom keeps those rooms comfortable because Nordstrom doesn't want customers to leave; Nordstrom wants customers to *stay*. Consequently, the company will do whatever it takes to keep that customer in the store, to continue to give him or her the opportunity to make purchases.

"The whole point of everything we do is to make the customer happy for the long haul," said David Lindsey, vice president of store planning. "If people are satisfied and excited about the experience of shopping at Nordstrom, they will come back. And if you haven't created that atmosphere, they won't come back. It's just that simple."

Food for Thought

Another way to keep people in the store is to feed them. Food and restaurant services have increasingly become an important attraction at Nordstrom. They generate profits while enhancing the shopping environment and, of course, give customers another reason not to leave the store.

Nordstrom has several in-store restaurant concepts, depending on the size and location of the individual store. The Espresso Bar (known as the eBar), which is usually located at an entrance outside the store, serves gourmet coffee drinks, Italian sodas, and pastries to Nordstrom customers as well as people walking through the mall. The Cafe serves soups, salads, sandwiches, pastries, and beverages. The Grill offers full-service dining of quick sandwiches, soups, salads, beer, wine, and full bar in an elegant atmosphere. This restaurant is very popular. If there is not a table ready for you, Nordstrom will take your reservation while you continue to shop. They give you, the customer, a beeper, promising to contact you when your table is ready.

Something Extra

In several of its larger stores, Nordstrom offers a concierge desk where shoppers receive special attention, whether it be helpful information about the store, a restaurant recommendation, or assistance in calling a cab. Need to check your coat, umbrella, and packages with the concierge? No problem.

The Customer Service department in each store offers check-cashing privileges for Nordstrom cardholders, immediate posting of payments to Nordstrom accounts, answers to inquiries regarding those accounts, monthly statements, credit line increases, complimentary gift wrapping, and purchase of gift certificates.

Some of the larger stores have a SPA Nordstrom, which offers natural aromatherapy, herbal body wrap, massage therapy, manicures, and aromatic facials. (Inexpensive shoeshines are available in the men's area of nearly all Nordstrom stores.)

Nordstrom also offers other features such as free gift boxes and a free personal shopping service, where a designated Nordstrom Personal Shopper will accompany the customer throughout the store to help with every purchasing decision.

Having created the kind of pleasant, inviting place where most women feel extremely comfortable, Nordstrom became the logical retailer to pioneer in-store mammograms at its store, in 1998, at the Old Orchard shopping center in Skokie, Illinois. The Breast Health and Mammography Center includes a state-of-the-art, low-dose mammography machine and film processor operated by staff from two local hospitals. The mammograms are read by radiologists at the hospitals and conveyed to the referring physicians' offices. Many rival department stores have since followed suit and are also offering mammograms.

As you're reading this, you're probably thinking: My business isn't set up for a concierge service, herbal body wraps, mammograms, or shoeshines. It doesn't have to be. But is your business set up for clean restrooms?

Several years ago, two female reporters from the *Washington Post* surveyed the ladies restrooms in all the department stores in the Washington, DC, area. Their criteria were all the things we look for in a good restroom—ample space and supplies, cleanliness, diaper-changing facilities, and so on. Nordstrom was rated Number One. GoCityKids, a web site in Los Angeles, specifically mentions the restrooms in its review of the Glendale Galleria: "Nordstrom's is particularly clean and has the most comfortable chairs for resting and nursing" ("GoCityKids: The City Guide for Parents," gocitykids.com.)

We don't usually associate clean restrooms with customer service, but why not? When your restrooms are clean and well supplied, you are telling your customer that you care about every aspect of their experience with your company.

Because parents with children also require more room, the dressing rooms and lounges (both men's and women's) are large enough to accommodate strollers and diaper-changing tables. Nearly all stores have special rooms for nursing mothers, and newer stores incorporate "family" bathrooms where a parent can accompany his or her child of the opposite sex. Some Nordstrom stores equip their children's areas with toys, coloring tables, television sets, video games, and built-in helium containers for blowing up balloons. In new markets, before a store is built, Nordstrom will sponsor a charity fundraiser that includes local children designing and signing their own floor tiles, which are later installed in the floor of the children's department of the store.

"All of these images, collectively, convey the personality of our store and what we are trying to be," said David Lindsey, vice president of store planning. "Everything we do is to enhance and romance the merchandise. The store is the backdrop with compelling merchandise taking center stage. Ultimately, because we are designing for a much longer time curve, we work to create a quality shopping environment—a special place that feels inviting, warm, and comfortable."

Emulating the Nordstrom Way

Several companies, which were featured in the previous book, *Lessons from The Nordstrom Way,* illustrate how businesses in various categories can devise clever ways to create an inviting place. Here are examples from a bank, a major airline, a regional medical facility, a world-class hotel, and a chain of car washes.

In every one of its more than 180 bank branches, FirstMerit Bancorporation, based in Akron, Ohio, features a receptionist whose primary purpose is to greet customers as they come in and offer assistance for whatever matters the customers need to resolve.

"By having a receptionist right out there in front, establishing eye contact, there is no question in the customer's mind as to where to go to get questions answered," said chairman and CEO John Cochran.

The interior of a FirstMerit branch does not conjure up the typical branch bank experience. The hues are bright; the chairs are comfortable, the displays for banking products are colorful. The teller line is located at the back of the branch so that customers walk past the product displays and the people who are selling those products. Partitions provide privacy for customers who want to conduct their business with their personal First-Merit banker.

"Our philosophy is that we want to emulate the whole Nordstrom interior feel of nice furnishings and finishes so that people feel that they are doing their business in a vibrant way with a company that invests in itself," said Cochran.

Continental Airlines allows its customers who are flying in first class to carry on an extra bag—an amenity that most other airlines frown upon.

"You have very rigid standards at other airlines," said retired chairman and CEO Gordon Bethune. "They have a one size fits all at a security checkpoint. So, regardless of the fact that you are a Platinum Elite first class ticket holder, you get the lowest common denominator on the baggage size. Do the math: There are four seats across in first class and six seats across in coach. So, in first class, you're paying for a seat and a half. So, why wouldn't you get the extra bag? We offer you that. We understand that you shouldn't worry that the materials you need for your presentation—or your underwear—might get lost if you had to check your baggage. We want to make sure you can have them both."

Bethune, a former executive at the Boeing Company convinced officials at the Seattle aircraft maker to back him on this stand. "That's why we bought bigger airplanes like the 777 with overhead bins that are bigger than the DC10s. That's what passengers want and we can safely store the bags. Why would we treat people on a 777 as if they were flying on a DC10? We don't have a winner and a loser with a baggage issue. We are not going to be at odds with our customer. We've attracted a huge ridership and the loyalty of people who want this consistent level in the way they are treated, taken to their destination on time, and the way we deliver their bags. Customers want and will pay for extra baggage space. We are going to provide that. Our employees understand that."

St. Charles Medical Center in Bend, Oregon, brought in experts from the Ritz-Carlton hotel chain to help to improve its food service. St. Charles's highly trained staff chefs prepare excellent cuisine from a selected menu, which can be brought to the rooms for all patients and visitors 24 hours a day. The kitchen responds to an order within 10 minutes.

Coincidentally, St. Charles uses Callison Architecture, the firm that has designed every Nordstrom store.

"We have spent a lot of money changing the physical environment of the hospital to reflect a welcoming place—having fresh flowers on the tables in the cafeteria and at every entrance to the hospital," said chairman and CEO emeritus Jim Lussier, who added that the biggest compliment anybody could give St. Charles "is that we do not look like a hospital. We've done our level best to not do that."

The second major change at St. Charles was in taking care of the human element.

"We used to take it for granted that most patients wanted to be here," said Lussier. "Well, guess what? We found out that they *didn't* want to be here. In fact, when they really got honest in surveys, they would tell us that the hospital is a really frightening place to be. Not only does their disease or illness take away a lot of their freedom, but as soon as they get to the hospital, we take away the rest of their freedom and dignity. We shave their head, we give them a number, we put a wrist band on them, we take away all of their clothes and give them a gown that's split down the back, and we say, 'Okay, we want you to be comfortable in this environment.' "

Today, if their condition allows it, patients can bring their own clothes from home and wear them for as long as they want in the presurgery orientation. They don't have to put on their hospital gown until they begin to get ready to go into surgery.

Wearing their own clothes makes patients "a whole lot more comfortable, while they are sitting in some sterile waiting area on a stretcher in front of God and everybody," added Lussier. "It completely transforms their mental orientation. Consequently, they are much more relaxed; they have less anxiety. They use less anesthesia. They recover quicker and they have fewer complications. These things are not just for convenience. They actually predetermine the psychological environment of the patient, and subsequently the clinical environment as well."

In virtually every major expansion and redesign project, St. Charles takes into consideration how the medical center can be more efficient and customer friendly. For example, after patients complained of being cold in the old surgery center, when the new surgery center was built, one of the features was a fireplace in the lobby. Besides obviously adding warmth, the fireplace "also completely changes the ambiance that is perceived by those patients coming in," said Lussier. "They fully expect to see something white, something sterile, something very unfriendly. We're trying to turn that perception upside down."

W Hotels and Westin Hotels, both divisions of Starwood Hotels & Resorts, feature the Heavenly Bed, which we consider the best hotel bed in America. Measuring 39.25 inches from the ground, the bed features an all-white thick down comforter, a12.5-inch pillow-top mattress (custom-made by Simmons); a thick, cozy down-filled feather bed, and dense 250-count sheets. When *Fortune* magazine rated various hotel beds, its reviewers gave the Heavenly Bed an A-plus rating, praising it as "fluffy, clean-looking, and incredibly comfortable." In 2003, Westin sold 2,000 fully loaded beds (pillows, sheets, comforter) for $2,990.00 each.

With so many parents traveling with small babies, W has been using special baby cribs as a differentiator between it and the competition.

"What's the most near and dear thing to people? Their children. Having traveled with children myself, I saw that you could niche yourself apart from your competitors if you just handled this component properly," said Tom Limberg, general manager of the W Hotel in Seattle. "Most of the baby cribs in hotels are beat up. They've been folded up so many times they're no longer a rectangle; they're a parallelogram. You don't know if they meet the latest safety standards for bar width. We bought the nicest chrome baby cribs we could find. And if you don't like one of those, we have the padded travel type that is built low to the floor. We have a pet bed that is feather filled as well. Our motto is that 'Everybody sleeps on the Heavenly Bed at W Seattle, whether you're on two legs or four.'"

Limberg believed that many hotels are "designed, built, and furnished to make life easier for the hotel and staff than for the guests." When that happens, the idea of that 'inviting place' takes a back seat to practicality and durability and ease of care.

A pleasing experience of an entirely different sort is what Mike's Express Carwash tries to give to its customers. Each of the chain's 28 units in Indiana and Ohio sits on an acre-plus of highly landscaped property, which is maintained by frequent lawn care and an underground sprinkling system. Mike's sites don't even look like a typical car wash. The handsome brick-and-glass buildings sometimes fool people into thinking that Mike's is actually a restaurant. Crews are constantly maintaining the cleanliness of the operation.

"We are in such an impulse-driven business," said Bill Dahm, Mike's president, "we have to have that nice clean image from the street."

Unlike the average car wash, Mike's is known as a place that entertains its clientele—particularly the children of its clientele. Giant, furry stuffed animals are placed strategically along the path that cars take on their way to getting clean. As kids look out the window of their parents' car, they get to see stuffed versions of Mickey Mouse, Minnie Mouse, Bert & Ernie, Big Bird, and Raggedy Ann, who are waving back to them.

"We try to take those opportunities—in the drying chamber, for example—for the kids to see something fun," said Dahm, whose father opened the first Mike's in 1948. "It's kind of a drive-by amusement park. At Halloween, we have a big budget to turn each location into a Halloween theme with scarecrows and cornstalks. We try to make it a fun experience. When I'm out socially and people learn I'm associated with Mike's, 9 times out of 10 they don't talk about how clean their car is; they talk about the stuffed animals."

Create an Inviting Web Site

But what if your business isn't a "place" at all? Perhaps it's a web site. It doesn't matter; the same principles apply. Is your web site easy to access? Does it take forever to download? Is your typeface easy to read? Easy to navigate? The great customer-service oriented web sites such as Amazon.com understand that they are not just selling *things*; they are involved in transactions, which will lead to other transactions. That's why their sites are inviting in every sense of the word.

There is no clearer example of online customer service than a web site that is simple, straightforward, and easy to navigate.

Your web site is a relationship channel with your customer; it is a crucial component to the fulcrum of a multichannel customer service strategy.

Your web site should be built around what your customers actually want to accomplish—not what you think might be technologically sexy. Because customers with varying levels of computer sophistication visit most web sites, companies should design their sites with neophytes in mind.

It's not critical or even necessary to be on the leading edge of technology. Many retailers want their site to be as familiar as other sites, just as most brick-and-mortar stores share the same basic physical format with other brick-and-mortar stores. After all, if you were designing a physical store, you wouldn't make it radically dissimilar from other stores; you wouldn't put the cash registers in the back; you wouldn't install departments that are not clearly identified.

Web Site Design: The KISS Principle Rules

Many web sites were initially the creation of people who understood the complexity of technology, but not of the simplicity of interaction between human beings. Those sites were festooned with cool technological doo-dads and graphics that often were not relevant to the experience. Nontechnical customers are looking for an intuitive experience. When they log on, they need to be taken by the hand, shown how to use the site, and how to navigate their way through the site. People like to be treated like people, even if they are online.

How quickly does your web site download? Do you use cute animation and flashy splash screens that are great for showing off, but not for doing business? Even in this age of DSL and Wi-Fi, build a web site that meets the needs of the customer who is still on the slowest dial up—because that shows sensitivity and re-spect for the customer by putting yourself in the shoes of your customers so that you can anticipate their every step. Virtually every department—not just marketing or information technol-ogy—in your organization should be involved in fine-tuning your web site.

Your home page is where you make your initial impression. It is the most crucial *touchpoint* to your customers. Consequently, you want that first page to be downloaded quickly. Online con-sumers have little patience to wait for a lazy-loading homepage. Can you imagine losing potential customers because they couldn't reach you on the telephone or couldn't push their way through the doors of your store?

Amazon.com's site has gone—and will continue to go—through many changes. Even though Amazon.com is a pure-play Internet retailer, its web site provides valuable lessons to multi-channel companies. When Amazon.com expanded its product line from purely books, CDs, DVDs, videos, and so on, it also added a bevy of new tabs. Eventually, the home page became a cluttered mess. For a while, the company cleaned up the muddle by reducing the main tabs down to two—"Welcome" and "Store Directory" and provided links to product categories, but they have since added more and more tabs. Nevertheless, Maryam Mohit, vice president of site design for Amazon, was spot-on when she told the *New York Times:* "When you come into a store, you need a soft landing where you can take a breath and orient yourself, as opposed to getting assaulted by a barrage of offers all at once. We wanted to create that soft landing online." Mohit added that her design team was influenced by the book *Why We Buy: The Science of Shopping,* by Paco Underhill, founder of Envirosell, a marketing research firm that studies shopping behavior. According to Underhill's book, "In the world of cyberspace, everywhere is an exit. You have the capacity to bail out at any point, and an enormous number of people do."

Consistency of purpose and design are prerequisites of a user-friendly web site. Customers feel comfortable negotiating a site that features elements that are consistent with other sites. Users want to be able to navigate the site as they feel, and not have to worry about retracing their steps, like Hansel and Gretel dropping bread crumbs to mark their trail back home.

Just as the door to your place of business should be easy to use, so should your web site. "Ease of use" should be your mantra.

Today's demanding customers want a site to provide attractive visuals, thorough product information, and straightforward communication. Throughout the experience, the help button must always be present and obvious. If there's a problem, customers want to be able to easily contact someone who can help them. A customer should be one click away from help by sending the company an e-mail, which should be answered within 24 hours, if not sooner. There should always be a phone number that is clearly posted, in case your customer requires additional assistance. Nordstrom.com's 800-number is easy to find on its web site. By comparison, you won't find an 800-number on the web sites of Macy's or Bloomingdale's.

Many online retailers believe the chances of retaining those customers markedly increase when they provide those customers with personal contact with a human connection, either through a toll-free telephone number or a live chat online. Even in today's wired world, most online customers prefer some form of human interaction during an e-commerce transaction. To those customers, it's not enough that a site offers direction through text-based information and frequently asked questions (FAQ). Nordstrom, like many other customer-friendly companies, have

CHAT or Help Button

FAQ SECTION

instituted a chat feature called "Live Help," which enables customers to communicate with knowledgeable customer service representatives. For example, Nordstrom discovered that one of the top 10 search phrases on nordstrom.com was for "Kate Spade," the designer of shoes and handbags. There was just one problem. At the time, Kate Spade shoes and handbags weren't available on nordstrom.com, but they were available at Nordstrom stores. So, to make sure the customer didn't leave the web site unhappy, Nordstrom redirected the customer to make a telephone call to a personal shopper in a Nordstrom store that carries the Kate Spade line. (Today, the Kate Spade line is available on nordstrom.com.)

Answer the Telephone!

That brings us to that staple of business tools: the telephone. The telephone can also help to create an inviting place. Today, the telephone is often a tool for exchanging voice mail messages, not for conducting an actual conversation. But even in the world of e-mail and web sites, the telephone is more important than ever.

How many times have you called a company and listened to a variation of the following message: "Thank you for calling ABC Company. Your call is important to us. Please note our menu has recently changed."

Do you care if the menu has changed? Chances are, you didn't know what the previous menu was.

As you listen to the menu, you find yourself evaluating which of those choices fits your particular question. If none of your choices is a perfect fit, you are then forced to replay the menu and then come up with the choice that most closely fits your problem. What is the result? A frustrated customer.

If you do have a person answering your phone (an increasingly rare occurrence), how does that person do his or her job? Does he or she have a pleasant voice? Does the voice reflect a smile? Does he or she sound helpful? *Is* he or she helpful? Can he or she supply answers to questions? Quite often, companies will just hire a warm body to answer that phone. Those companies are sabotaging themselves. The person who answers your phone is your public voice, the voice that tells your customers that you want their business and will do whatever it takes to win their trust.

PUBLICIST

"Creating an inviting place" means devising a place—store, office, web site—that best serves the customer. Nordstrom has succeeded by thinking like the customer. The company's web site offers help 24/7. At all full-line stores, real people answer the phones during store hours; you never get a recorded message telling you that your call is important. Nordstrom proves twenty-four hours a day, seven days a week, that when you think like the customer, you will never go wrong.

Do A phone meeting for STAFF.

Keys to Success

How can we expect customers to buy what we're offering when we haven't made them feel comfortable by being attentive to every detail of the experience? Whether your business is bricks-and-mortar or virtual, stationary or in motion, temporary or permanent, you need to create an inviting place where it is a pleasure to do business:

- Make your public voice or face a pleasant one.
- Create an atmosphere of helpfulness.
- Create an atmosphere of professionalism.

(Continued)

(Continued)

- Create a place that's clean and attractive.

- Make your guests feel that they are a part of your environment.

- Provide a consistent experience across all channels

- Create a web site that is simple, straightforward, and easy to navigate.

- Because customers with varying levels of computer sophistication visit most web sites, design your site with the least sophisticated user in mind.

- In web site design, the KISS Principle rules.

- Use your site to help educate the customer.

- The most user-friendly web sites have been designed and re-designed based on the feedback received from users.

- Continually add features and services, which add value to your web site.

EXERCISE

You're the Customer

Is your place of business an "inviting place"? Do you make customers feel that they are important? It's easy to find the answers to those questions.

- Select several people in your organization and give them this assignment:

(Continued)

(Continued)

- Walk into your place of business as if you've never been there before. Pretend *you* are the customer. Write down the following:

  —What do you see?
  —What *don't* you see?
  —Is everything clearly marked?
  —Is there someone there to help you?
  —What do you like?
  —What don't you like?
  —What would you like to change?

- After everyone has completed this assignment, reconvene the group and compare your answers. Clearly, if everyone is finding similar problems, it is time to address those problems.

- Assign some of the people in the group to institute changes that make your business a customer-friendly place.

EXERCISE

Call Your Company

As in the previous exercise, pretend you are a customer.

- Call your company, as if you were a customer.

- Ask to speak to a particular person whom you know is out of the office.

(Continued)

(Continued)

- Ask a question about a product or service.

- Make notes on what works and what doesn't.

- Again, as in the previous exercise, reconvene your colleagues to compare notes, and then find ways to improve the answering of your telephone and your entire telephone system.

EXERCISE

Surf Your Company's Web Site

- Gather people who work in all aspects of your business to evaluate the efficiency and customer-friendly qualities of your web site.

- Where are all of the places where people are likeliest to abandon your web site?

- Again, as in the previous exercises, reconvene your colleagues to compare notes, and then find ways of making your web site more customer-friendly.

4

How Can I Help You?

Provide Your Customers with Lots of Choices

How do I love thee? Let me count the ways.

—Robert Browning

B ack in 1915, Henry Ford was reported to have said that his customers could buy a Model T Ford in any color they liked—just as long as it was black. There was a reason for that: Ford sold only black cars because black enamel paint was the fastest-drying paint available at that time; pigmented colors required a much longer drying period. Thus, black enamel was the ideal paint for Ford's revolutionary assembly-line production because a dry car body was ready to mount on a chassis and be sold as soon as possible. Even when other fast-drying colors became available, Ford stuck with black for more than a decade, so as not to slow down the production process.

Henry Ford made a classic mistake—a mistake that many companies, large and small, continue to make to this day: creating a business model that is structured to make life easier for the company, not for the customer. For many years, Ford's company produced only one model of automobile; the company didn't introduce a new design, the Model A, until 1927. But by that time, rivals such as General Motors were flourishing because they were offering consumers alternatives.

Today's consumers have more choices than ever. The choices you offer your customers represent a competitive edge that you will have over your rivals.

Wide and Deep Inventories _____

At Nordstrom, the most obvious illustration of choice is the company's longstanding commitment to stocking its stores with a *wide* selection and *deep* inventories—a compelling combination of world renown brands and Nordstrom's own brands—that are broader than the selection offered by Nordstrom's peer stores. Although this way of doing business is costly—it's expensive to own that much inventory—Nordstrom, almost from the time it began in 1901 as a modest shoe store, has always operated on the belief that if it offered its customers a vast *length, breadth,* and *depth* of wares, customers would be less likely to walk out of the store without making a purchase—or two or three. (In recent years, Nordstrom has made great strides in better managing its inventory, which has helped to hold down costs and produce better profit margins.)

Back in Nordstrom's earliest days, when co-founders John W. Nordstrom and Carl F. Wallin—both neophytes in the footwear business—ran the fledgling enterprise, "The store was so small and looked so poor that the fellows from the better factories back East wouldn't even call on us to sell us shoes," John W. told the *Seattle Post-Intelligencer* in a 1961 interview commemorating the store's 60th anniversary.

Starting out at the beginning of the twentieth century, Nordstrom and Wallin made their initial purchasing decisions by relying on the advice of traveling salesmen. At first, because neither man knew much about merchandising, they simply bought shoes in all the medium-size ranges because they figured that this simple approach would satisfy the large majority of customers. But soon, John W. would later claim, they discovered that those sizes were not large enough for their strapping, big-boned fellow immigrant Swedes who had settled in Seattle. Consequently, they began purchasing shoes that would better fit those customers. That story may be apocryphal, but Wallin & Nordstrom did begin carrying larger sizes, and soon established a reputation for their breadth of inventory, a reputation that continues to this day.

"To get customers to leave Frederick & Nelson or The Bon Marche [the then-prominent downtown Seattle department stores] and go to our store, they had to do everything right," said John N. Nordstrom, the retired co-chairman of the company. As a young boy, John N. a grandson of John W., worked in the store with his grandfather; his father, Elmer; his uncles, Everett and Lloyd; his brother Jim; and his cousin Bruce. "Better not miss a size, better be nice, and have the right styles. My generation [John N., Bruce, Jim, and Jack McMillan, who ran the company from the late 1960s to the mid-1990s] copied that system. We didn't try to have only the biggest selection or the best prices; we had to do everything."

Because Nordstrom continues to want to attract people of all shapes and sizes, the company remains committed to carrying more sizes—particularly in footwear—than any comparable retailer. A typical Nordstrom store carries upwards of 75,000 pairs of shoes, with the world's widest selection (under one roof) of sizes and widths—from women's shoes in sizes 4 to 14 and widths aa to ww, and men's shoes in sizes 5 to 20 and widths aa to eeeeee—in a broad range of styles and colors. Unlike much of the competition, the store carries many half sizes, which help to ensure a better fit. When a customer has over a size-and-a-half difference between foot sizes, it has long been a Nordstrom practice to split sizes so that the customer doesn't have to buy two full pair of shoes.

After they have measured the customer's feet, Nordstrom salespeople are trained to show customers several shoe options.

"For someone with hard-to-fit feet, we like our salespeople to come out of the backroom with as many as 8 or 10 or 12 pairs of shoes," said Jack Minuk, vice president of women's shoes. "To see the response from that customer—who has probably had difficulty finding shoes that fit her—when a salesperson comes out with literally armloads of shoes, is a remarkable experience."

That's why Nordstrom maintains its wide and deep inventories.

"The only way to truly fit a customer is by having sizes," added Minuk. "The reality is that most people don't fit into a small box of sizes. They settle for a shoe that in many cases doesn't fit them well. So, if we truly believe in perfect fit, we can only do that by having an extended range of sizes and widths."

Nordstrom is also committed to providing customers with choices in every aspect of its business. In apparel, the retailer offers a broad array of sizes, from petite to plus-sizes in women's fashions, and short to extra-extra-large tall clothes for men. Quite often, the company will reinforce this idea of choice in its advertisements. One newspaper ad shows four distinctly different looking men having a business meeting. One man is tall; another is short; one is stocky; another is thin. The headline reads: "Every man deserves a great looking, great fitting suit." The point is very clear: Whatever your size or shape, we've got the suit that will be perfect for you.

This idea of choice also extends to other facilities in the store. For example, Nordstrom's stores offer several different kinds of restaurants, from an espresso to a full-service restaurant, because Nordstrom wants to wrap its collective arms around the customers and never let them go. Lots of choices make those arms stretch out a little bit farther.

The Right Choices at the Right Time _____

John N. Nordstrom's late brother, Jim, once said, "There's nothing more demoralizing for a salesperson than to not be able to satisfy the customer. Our number-one responsibility to our salespeople is to have the products that the customers want when the customers come into the store. You can have all the pep rallies in the world, but the best motivation is stocking the right item in the right size at the right price."

Bob Middlemas, who today is executive vice president and Central States regional manager (overseeing 11 stores in 7 states), learned that lesson early in his career, when he was a buyer of men's tailored clothing in Nordstrom's Oregon region. When Middlemas's merchandise manager was on sick leave, Bob filled in for several weeks. "One day, I'm sitting at my desk and I get a phone call from John [N.] Nordstrom. That got my attention," Middlemas recalled. "He said, 'Bob, I was out visiting your region the last few days. I went to the men's furnishings department of your Clackamas Town Center store [outside of Portland, Oregon] and I noticed that you didn't have any 17½ [neck], 35-inch [sleeve] white shirts. And your tall-men's tie selection looks very, very weak, considering what a trend that is in our men's furnishings business right now. Could you check on that and get back to me?' "

Middlemas immediately got on the case. After making some inquiries, he came up with a clear, simple answer to the question posed to him by the man every employee calls "Mr. John": The distribution center was out of size 17½, 35-inch white shirts, but a new delivery was expected in a couple of weeks. The neckwear manufacturer said that the tall-men's ties were on their way to the distribution center and would be in the stores in a few days. The young Middlemas, eager to please his boss, felt proud of

75

himself, "because I thought I had done my job. I called Mr. John back and said, 'I got the answers you were looking for,'" and proceeded to tell him about the inventory that was on its way to the distribution center.

But Middlemas did not receive the response he was expecting. In fact, his explanation was met with stony silence on the other end of the telephone line. Finally, Mr. John replied: "Bob, you didn't understand my question. I didn't ask you *where* they were. I asked you *why* we didn't have them." The point, Middlemas realized, "was that I should figure out a way to solve the problem. If we don't have the stock, we should get it from one of our vendors so we don't walk [lose] a customer on a thirty-five-dollar dress shirt. Because if we walk him on the dress shirt, we're not going to sell him the shoes or the tie or the belt, and he's going to be disappointed in our company."

This kind of attitude and philosophy are ingrained in the Nordstrom culture. Forty years before Mr. John taught Bob Middlemas a valuable lesson, John's uncle, Everett (known as "Mr. Everett") did something similar for one of his shoe buyers. When Everett asked the buyer why a size 7B in a certain style was not in stock, the buyer replied that it was on order. Everett asked for a copy of the order sheet. He folded it up, put it in a shoebox, and placed the box on a shelf in the stockroom. "Now," he told the buyer, "when the customer for that size 7B comes into the store, tell her to try that order on."

"Everybody Should Have Lots of Choices"

In other words, no excuses. The only way you can protect yourself from losing a customer to your competition is to make sure you have all the choices you need to make sure that you can satisfy that customer.

This commitment to satisfying the customer came into sharp relief in the spring of 2004 when a letter from a young customer arrived at the Nordstrom corporate headquarters in Seattle. The letter was from Ella Gunderson, who wrote:

Dear Nordstrom,

I am an 11-year-old girl who has tried shopping at your store for clothes (in particular jeans), but all of them ride way under my hips, and the next size up is too big and falls down. I see all of these girls who walk around with pants that show their belly button and underwear. Your clearks sugjest [sic] that there is only one look. If that is true, then girls are suppose to walk around half naked. I think that you should change that.

Ella's letter was relayed all the way up to Pete Nordstrom, executive vice president of the company and president of the full-line store division. Kris Allan, manager of Nordstrom's store in the Bellevue Square shopping mall, across Lake Washington from Seattle, where Ella shopped, wrote back to Ella, promising the girl from the Seattle suburb of Redmond, that the company would let its buyers and salespeople know that young customers wanted more choices in fashion, rather than just the hot look of the moment. Kris Allan wrote: "Wow. Your letter really got my attention. . . . I think you are absolutely right. There should not be just one look for everyone. This look is not particularly a modest one and there should be choices for everyone."

The story doesn't stop there. A reporter for the *Seattle Times* wrote an article about Ella's letter and Nordstrom's enthusiastic response. Soon after, other newspapers around the country picked up the story or wrote their own version. Because Ella attended a Catholic school, several national Catholic publications, newsletters, and web sites ran similar stories. The national political columnist Michelle Malkin, giving a speech in July 2004, to Clare Booth Luce Policy Institute's Conservative Leadership Seminar in Washington, said: "As the mother of a 4-year-old girl and an 8-month-old boy, I am increasingly dismayed by the liberal assault on decency, the normalization of promiscuity, and the mainstream media's role as shameless collaborators. First, let me tell you about my new hero. Her name is Ella Gunderson . . ."

Ella and her mom were later flown to New York, where they appeared with Pete Nordstrom on CNN and on the *Today* show on NBC. In an interview with Katie Couric, Ella told a national television audience, "There can be more than one look. Everybody should have lots of choices." Pete Nordstrom explained to *Today* show viewers that customer letters help the company listen, be responsive, and fulfill its commitment to carry a wide variety of styles. He also said that Nordstrom had already addressed the issue of modest clothing, but that the Ella story was a good reminder.

Nordstrom.com

When Nordstrom launched Nordstrom.com in the late 1990s, the company proclaimed the site as the "World's Largest Shoe Store," offering over two million pairs of shoes, and almost 400,000 stock-keeping units of apparel and shoes for men, women, and children.

The site presents an appealing menu of features to personalize the online experience for each shopper. The web page can be customized so that customers can store their personal size information and personal preferences.) They have the option of either ordering from the web site or from the Nordstrom catalog.

Nordstrom enhances the site by providing live chat with customer service representatives between 5 A.M. and 11:30 P.M. Pacific time. Customers can also either e-mail or use the 800-number to speak to a Nordstrom representative.

Shoppers have the option to do what Nordstrom calls "power browse"—which allows shoppers to click on several main categories to find items they are looking for. For example, customers can find items by using pull-down menus that allow them to select a product category (men's apparel, women's shoes, etc.), sub-category (suits, sweaters, etc.), brand, size, and color. Once all those options are selected, customers can immediately locate what they are looking for. On the consumer web site *epinions.com,* a woman talked about buying a holiday dress on Nordstrom.com. She wrote: "The Nordstrom's web site is so well organized, I was able to narrow my dress choices down quickly, even in the midst of a 'What was I thinking?' panic." She merely had to make three quick clicks: (1) "women," (2) "festive attire," and (3) "easy elegance" and, she continued, "Poof—60 choices over four pages. I found five dresses I liked in a matter of minutes and added them to my shopping cart."

NPlus

Nordstrom has encapsulated its variety of choices and points-of-difference under the heading of "NPLUS: the extras you deserve!" These include:

- *We stand behind everything we sell.*
  If you're not happy with your purchase, simply bring it back.

- *We have on-site tailors.*
  Expert tailoring and alterations are available with any purchase.
- *We provide prosthesis products and services.*
  We're here to help with your post-mastectomy needs, including the processing of insurance information.
- *We assure you'll never pay more.*
  If you find the same item for a lower price, we will gladly match that price.
- *We have live operators to answer your call.*
  When you call us during store hours, one of our Nordstrom employees will answer in person—right away. We also have a Credit Call Center at your service, 24/7. Have a question about your account, Nordstrom Rewards™ points, an upcoming event, or store hours and locations? Our specialists are ready to assist you.
- *We search to find what you want.*
  If we don't have the item you want, we'll track it down from one of our other stores or online at Nordstrom.com.
- *We stock more sizes.*
  From shoes to clothes to intimate apparel, our size selection is far beyond average. And if we don't have your size in stock, we'll make every effort to find it.
- *We have certified fit experts.*
  Our Certified Shoe Fitters and Fit Specialists in Lingerie are trained to exacting standards. Plus, we have trained experts in cosmetics, skincare, and fragrance.
- *We offer complimentary gift boxes.*
  Available with every purchase, at every sales counter.
- *We're family friendly.*
  Nordstrom is a great place to bring the whole family. You'll find a full children's menu and coloring sheets in our café,

a family restroom, and a mother's room. Strollers and wheel-chairs are readily available, and roomy aisles make browsing our store easy.

Emulating the Nordstrom Way

Many companies do a great job of offering a Nordstrom-style selection of choices and service. One example is FirstMerit Corporation, a bank catering to small- and medium-sized businesses in the very concentrated northeast Ohio marketplace. These customers need the same wide array of banking options that are required by businesses of much bigger size.

To help employees feel comfortable explaining the company's wide range of financial products, all of the employees involved in selling the various bank products are assembled as teams and are taught each other's business, including a broad and detailed understanding of the features and benefits of each product and service that a corporate customer would need. They are taught how to identify that need and how to speak to the benefits of that product.

In the hotel business, Tom Limberg, manager of W Seattle, said, "We've charged ourselves with the responsibility of being someone's home away from home," but with virtually no knowledge of what that home is all about. Consequently, "we have to have the ability to provide choices and offer alternatives. Our philosophy is to stay away from the 'N' word ('No'). We hate the 'N' word."

Providing alternatives—choices—is the best way to stay away from saying "No" to the customer. If you can't provide "A," perhaps you can provide "B."

W Hotel's customer service department, is called Whatever Whenever. "That is our service mentality. That's what they do," said Limberg.

The first week W Seattle was opened in 1999, a guest wanted to plug his laptop into the in-room high-speed Internet access port at the desktop. One problem: He had forgotten to bring his Ethernet connector.

"It was very frustrating for him," said Limberg. "Linc, our lead Welcome Ambassador (the equivalent to a bell captain), was very computer literate. He searched around and finally found an Ethernet connector on one of the laptops that we use in our purchasing department, and we brought it up to the guest's room. Not having that connector knocked purchasing out of the water for a few hours, but that was okay because it happened at the waning part of their day. Most importantly, we rallied for the customer and provided him with what he needed."

As happy as he was to find a solution, Limberg was just as pleased that an employee was comfortable going into the administrative offices to get some results.

As a result of that episode, the hotel created "our little inventory of things like that for Whatever Whenever, so that in the future we can more easily accommodate those types of requests."

My favorite Continental Airlines' choice is the option to carry on a luggage bag that is bigger than those being restricted by the other major carriers. Years ago, retired chairman and CEO Gordon Bethune was moved to make that decision when he was flying out of the San Diego airport and witnessed a confrontation between security guards and a Continental passenger over the size of a bag that was too large, according to the baggage "sizer" that was installed by Delta Airlines, which managed the security contract for the concourse Continental used at the airport. Continental ticket agents ultimately escorted the passenger through security by explaining that the bag conformed to Continental's more generous specifications. If you fly a lot and prefer to carry on your luggage, that's a choice you appreciate.

Keys to Success

The best customer service companies provide their clients with a wide range of options because the more options the more likely the customer will want to do business with you, rather than your competition. Are you providing your customers with choices, or are you a one-size-fits-all business?

- Examine the choices you offer your customers.
- Evaluate whether those choices are adequate to delight your customers.
- Examine the choices your competition offers your customers and respond to that difference.
- Use enhanced customer choices as a sales tool as well as a customer relationship builder.
- Make sure all your employees are aware of—and can readily offer and talk about—all of your choices.
- Provide customers with alternatives—rather than having to offer a flat "No."
- Provide your customers with multiple—and effective—ways to contact you.
- Educate your customer to make sound choices.
- Figure out what choices the customer is willing to pay for.

EXERCISE

Expand Your Customers' Choices

When Robert Spector conducts brainstorming exercises with his clients, the most popular customer service principle is "Provide Your Customers with Choices." For example, in a session with employees of a California-based company that specializes in building urban housing, the firm's frontline people came up with a long list of new choices that they knew their customers would appreciate. Their ideas covered everything from the products and services they offered to the hours they were open for business. These ideas included:

- Designer-selected packages of color-coordinated paint, tile, and flooring.

- Extended and flexible weekend and evening hours.

- Offering additional option packages on their web site.

What kind of ideas can you come up with for your company and your customers?

This exercise is divided into five parts. Select every aspect of your organization in which customer options are available, including:

1. Products.

2. Services.

3. Commercial channels, include brick-and-mortar operations, web sites, telephones, or catalogs.

4. Communication channels, including telephone, e-mail, and snail mail.

(Continued)

(Continued)

5. Means of payment, including credit cards, lines of credit, installment terms.

■ Generate a list of all the new options (that you currently do not offer) which might delight your customers in each of these categories and subcategories.

■ Make sure that everyone in every aspect of your organization has an opportunity to contribute to this list.

■ Pull together a team to help each department implement the best ideas from the list.

■ Distribute a list of the new customer options to all members of your organization.

PART II

WHAT SUPERVISORS CAN DO TO CREATE NORDSTROM-STYLE SERVICE

P art II examines the area of influence of the people closest to frontline service providers. These responsibilities include hiring the right people, then empowering, managing, mentoring, praising, rewarding, and retaining those people. As most of us know, senior managers create the atmosphere and the culture, but it is up to the people on the frontlines to do the rest.

This is particularly true at Nordstrom, where virtually every manager—including people who happen to have the last name Nordstrom—begin their career on the selling floor, before they rise up through the ranks. Nordstrom employees, regardless of whether they rose up through the ranks to become managers or chose to remain as frontline salespeople, universally appreciate the company's promote-from-within policy because it creates a culture where every manager and every buyer has gone through the same experiences as the people he or she is managing. No one manages until he or she has "walked in the shoes" of those managed.

Clear evidence of this culture of upward mobility is that only 2 of 36 corporate officers came from outside the company; all of the others rose from the stock room and the selling floor.

Because they have experienced every level of the organization, Nordstrom's best frontline managers know what to look for in a new hire, and they know how to empower those people, mentor them, recognize them, and praise them for a job well done. In this part of the book, we learn how Nordstrom managers do that and how you can use these same tools to empower, mentor, recognize, and praise the people who work with you and for you.

Praise
Empower
Recognize
Mentor

5

Nordstrom's #1 Customer Service Strategy

Hire the Smile

Character and personal force are the only investments that are worth anything.

—Walt Whitman

In the 1920s and 1930s, when they began to expand their business, John W. Nordstrom's three sons—Everett, Elmer, and Lloyd—created a sales-driven entrepreneurial culture by recruiting "fiery producers, tough guys, men who had to work hard to put bread on the table," Elmer once said. Hiring these self-described "shoe dogs," who were attracted to the Nordstrom system where employees earned commissions on each and every shoe sale, "was usually a shot in the dark," added Elmer. "In most cases, we just looked them over, gave them a shoe horn, and watched how they performed."

Even though Elmer (the last-surviving second generation Nordstrom, who died in 1993 at the age of 89) was describing the Nordstrom philosophy of more than eight decades ago, that philosophy still holds true today. A can-do attitude, a positive personality, and a strong work ethic are still the primary ingredients for success at Nordstrom. Some things will never change.

The qualities that Nordstrom looks for in its employees couldn't be more basic. First of all, the company wants its salespeople to be *nice*.

"We can hire nice people and teach them to sell," current chairman Bruce Nordstrom likes to say, "but we can't hire salespeople and teach them to be nice."

The Nordstrom corollary to that philosophy is "hire the smile, train the skill."

Learning that Nordstrom provides little in the way of a formalized training program, Robert Spector once asked Mr. Bruce: "Then who trains your salespeople?" His simple answer: "Their parents."

"Okay," you're probably asking, "what company or organization *doesn't* want to hire nice, motivated people?"

Of course, they all do. The difference is that Nordstrom and other great customer service companies want to hire people who are *already* nice and *already* motivated to do a good job *before* they walk through the door to apply for a job.

Have you ever tried to make someone who is not inherently nice actually be nice? It can't be done. Isn't it amazing how many times during the course of our day we cross paths with people who deal with the public, but are not nice. These people, who are the public voice or public face of a company or an organization, often give the impression that they just don't like people. You want to shake them by the shoulders and yell, "Find another line of work! Become a lighthouse keeper, but don't work in a job where you have to deal with people!"

Nordstrom believes the key to good customer service is to hire good people and keep working with them, nurturing them, and giving them the tools that they need to succeed, including attractive, inviting stores; high-quality merchandise, a wide range of product choices and sizes, and customer-friendly policies such as the Nordstrom return policy, which is virtually an unconditional, no-questions-asked, money-back feature.

Previous retail experience has never been a prerequisite for getting hired at Nordstrom. In fact, if a job applicant has already worked in retail, that experience might be a detriment because the applicant may have developed bad customer-service habits, such as reflexively saying "no" to the customer, rather than "yes."

A college degree has never been a prerequisite for succeeding at Nordstrom. Enthusiasm, a desire to work hard, and a capacity to generate your own traffic are much more important in a system that can best be described as a process of natural selection—a survival of the fittest that is purely Darwinian.

At Nordstrom, new employees are put out there on the sales floor and are expected to grasp the values and expectations of the culture, and either they catch it or they don't. They have to prove to management—and to themselves—that they really believe in helping others and genuinely like to give customer service.

"Some people who work at Nordstrom may find that they are in the wrong job," said McCarthy. "If sales aren't for you, but you like the company, Nordstrom will find a place for you as a support person. We don't want to lose people who have been with the company for several years because they understand the culture." McCarthy, like several others who eventually become top sales performers, didn't achieve immediate success. It wasn't until his seventh year with the company that everything came together for him and his business began to bloom.

Top salespeople come from all walks of life. Some join the company from other retailers (providing they did not pick up bad habits). Others come from other walks of life. But they bring with themselves a strong desire to give great customer service.

- David Butler, a retired self-described modern day "shoe dog," who started in the Nordstrom store in Tacoma, Washington, just out of high school in 1968, when the department manager, Butler recalled, "gave me a shoehorn and said, 'Let's see what you can do.'"
- Kazumi Ohara, manager of the Chanel boutique in the downtown Seattle store, used to work for an insurance company.

■ Pat McCarthy, Nordstrom's all-time top salesperson, first joined the company in 1972 after working for several years as a youth corrections counselor.

Leslie Umagat, who works in the Brass Plum juniors department in the downtown Seattle store, practically grew up in the Nordstrom organization. The Seattle native first went to work for the company in 1994 as a member of the Brass Plum Fashion Board, which is comprised of high school seniors. Applicants are judged on merit, volunteer activities, and scholastic grades and selected by Brass Plum department managers, buyers, and salespeople.

"As a Nordstrom customer, I wanted to be on the Brass Plum Fashion Board because it was a cool thing to be a part of. It was something different that you couldn't find elsewhere," she recalled.

From there, Leslie worked in the Brass Plum department as a stock person during summers and special sales. "I was raised in Brass Plum," she said with a grin.

Eventually, she became a part-time cashier, and then when she enrolled at the University of Washington in Seattle, she became a full-time salesperson, continuing after graduating from the University.

Bob Love

A list of the kind of people who succeed at Nordstrom wouldn't be complete without a mention of Bob Love.

Back in the 1970s, the 6'8" Love was one of the top players in the National Basketball Association. He played 11 seasons, most of them with the Chicago Bulls, and was the team's leading scorer for seven straight years. Before Michael Jordan came along, Love held all of the Bulls' scoring records, and was a three-time NBA All-Star. Toward the end of his career, he was traded to the Seattle SuperSonics. After hurting his back, Love was forced to retire. He went through much adversity, losing his money, his wife, and much of his self-respect. To compound his troubles, Love had a severe stutter, which had kept him from being able to endorse products or to be interviewed by the media. In the early 1980s, after seven years of trying to find a steady job, he found himself busing tables and washing dishes in the restaurant in the Nordstrom flagship store in downtown Seattle, Washington, where he was paid $4.45 an hour.

It was hard to miss this 6′8″ black man cleaning tables. Love could overhear the whispers: "Hey, that's Bob Love. He used to be a great basketball player. What a shame."

After working for year and a half at Nordstrom, Love was taken aside by co-chairman John N. Nordstrom, who praised Love's work and, more importantly, told him that the only way he was going to advance in the company was if he could find a way to deal with his speech impediment. John N. Nordstrom offered to help pay for Love's speech training. Eventually, for the first time in his life, Love could speak without stuttering. He ultimately rose up through the ranks to become a diversity affairs manager for Nordstrom until he was hired by the Chicago Bulls to become director of community affairs. And, even more impressive is the fact that, today, Bob Love is a highly sought-after inspirational and motivational speaker.

It's Not a Job for Everyone

For many years, Betsy Sanders was vice president and general manager for Nordstrom's Southern California division. As a retail industry leader in Southern California, she frequently met with her regional competitors for United Way meetings and the like, and on those occasions, she would invariably be taken aside by one of her competitors, who wanted to know, confidentially, where Nordstrom found all those gung-ho salespeople who enjoyed working in a hotly competitive system.

"Those retailers never got it," recalled Sanders, now a retail consultant and a former long-time member of the board of directors of Wal-Mart Stores, Inc. "We got our people from the same employee pool they did. The difference between Nordstrom and its competitors was that the Nordstroms didn't go around talking about how wretched their people were. The Nordstroms thought they had great people. And look at the result."

To this day, the company has very high expectations "and if you don't make it, you're out of there," added Sanders. "People would ask me if it was true that if you don't do a good job at Nordstrom you're gone. I'd say, 'Yes, I hope so.'"

Van Mensah, who sells men's suits in the suburban Washington, DC, Pentagon City (Virginia) store, is often asked to speak to new employees at Nordstrom. One of the top-performing salespeople in the chain for almost two decades, Van doesn't sugarcoat the demands of the job.

"Demands and expectations are high, but if you like working in an unrestricted environment, it's a great place to work," he explained. "Nordstrom provides you with great merchandise and the freedom to do what you want. I always tell people that if you're interested in retail, this is the best place to work. But you have to understand that this is not for everybody. It's a tough job, but if you have the discipline and you are willing to work hard and take the initiative, it's not that tough. After a while, it becomes easy, because you get used to so many things. It becomes a habit. With the tools and the resources the company provides, there's no reason for anybody not to make it."

Len Kuntz, the vice president and regional manager of Washington/Alaska, who has opened several stores and interviewed many people in his 20-year career at Nordstrom, opines that people come to work for the company for four reasons:

1. Opportunity for growth.
2. Freedom. ("There are almost no barriers to doing your job," said Kuntz.)
3. Feeling that you are part of something meaningful. ("Selling clothes isn't what we do," said Kuntz. "It's filling people's needs and making them feel better emotionally.")
4. Feeling valued. ("The more people are valued, the more connected they become. It perpetuates itself.")

Good Place to Work

Nordstrom has consistently been selected as one of the 100 Best Companies to Work for in America. More than 3,000 of its employees have been there for more than 10 years. It is among the top 50 companies in the United States based on wages of women corporate officers, who constitute more than 40 percent of corporate officers.

Nordstrom has set up a compensation system to help employees achieve personal wealth. The company has a generous 401 (k) plan as well as profit sharing and an employee stock-purchase plan.

Like everything else at Nordstrom, the profit-sharing plan has built-in financial incentives that encourage industriousness, teamwork, customer service, and expense savings. Because contributions are made to the plan directly from the company's net earnings, employees have an incentive to be productive and cost-conscious. (Nordstrom's shrinkage rate—losses due to employee theft—is only a little less than 2 percent of sales.) That also promotes loyalty because employees share ownership. Today, some longtime employees retire with profit-sharing totals in the high six figures. All employees who work more than a thousand hours per year and are still actively employed at the end of the year participate in the plan.

New Employees in New Markets

As Nordstrom expands across America, the company faces a constant challenge of finding the kind of people who want to give Nordstrom-like service. For every 300 or 400 positions that Nordstrom needs to fill in a new store, the company usually receives some 3,000 or 4,000 applicants; in other words, a person has a 1 in 10 chance of getting hired at Nordstrom.

The people who are not hired are sent thank you notes because their effort to apply is appreciated and, after all, Nordstrom would like them to remain or become Nordstrom customers.

Bob Middlemas, who opened the Midwest division for Nordstrom in the 1990s, said, "We knew that the most important thing we had to accomplish was to hire Nordstrom kind of people. What does that mean? We talked about what makes someone successful at Nordstrom. What do we look for? A nice person who is friendly, likes people, likes making people happy, wants to have someone leave the store saying, wow, what a great person; what great service."

When Denise Barzcak interviewed for a job at Nordstrom's new Boca Raton (Florida) store in the Town Center Mall, she discovered the company was just as interested in her experiences in life as it was in her experiences in retail. (She had previously worked for Ann Taylor and Casual Corner in her native Western New York.)

"They really made you think back to your life experiences," she recalled. "They want to know what kind of person you are. They don't talk a lot about customer service. With the very first interviews, they chose people who were already naturally good at customer service. You can probably train anyone to do the systems part of it—the register, the ticketing, the merchandise—but you can't teach people to be friendly or great with people."

Denise recalled how veteran employees who had come to Florida to open and work in the new store would stand up and speak about their own history, where they had started, and where they had worked before.

"So many people said, 'I started with Nordstrom when I was in college and that originally it was a part-time job,' but they were still working for the company," recalled Denise, who moved from selling women's apparel in the Town Center Mall to a position as a buyer in the Dallas Galleria store. "There was such a great retention rate and so many great success stories. That was really encouraging. All the people who work for Nordstrom have this passion about the business. You really feel that they believe in what they are saying. That's inspiring. When you are sitting there listening to it, you get excited because they are so excited."

As we will see in the exercises at the conclusion of this chapter, when interviewing prospective employees, it is important to ask probing questions to draw out information about applicants' attitude and aptitude for customer service. Nevertheless, as Blake Nordstrom says: "We don't have a standard set of interview questions. We don't want to be homogenized."

Diversity

Nordstrom has had a longstanding commitment to increase the minority representation in its general employee and management ranks. Company policy is to reach out to their communities to recruit, employ, train, and promote ethnic and racial minorities.

In 1988, 15.7 percent of Nordstrom managers were people of color; in 2004, that figure was 26.4 percent. In 1988, 23.9 percent of the entire Nordstrom workforce were people of color; today that number is 39.1 percent. Among the 104 company officers, 56 are women and 13 percent are people of color. Three people of color and two women also serve on the board of directors.

Throughout this period, Nordstrom has consistently had a workforce that consisted of more than 70 percent women.

Nordstrom actively pursues the recruitment of a multicultural/multiethnic workforce through job fairs, community organizations, and college placement centers. Minority employment figures are tracked regularly for each region in the company.

In 2004, *Fortune* magazine, in its June 28, 2004 issue, ranked Nordstrom Number 27 among the "50 Best Companies for Minorities" in the U.S., up from Number 33 for the year before.

The company routinely conducts sensitivity training for employees that focuses on diversity issues in the workplace.

To recruit workers with disabilities, company representatives attend special job fairs and work with businesses, service agencies, and assistive technology providers who network with the disabled community.

Nordstrom is perennially selected to the Hispanic 100, a group of companies catering to that community. Nordstrom is considered the first upscale retailer to advertise in *Ebony,* a magazine that caters to African Americans, and also advertises in *Essence, Hispanic Business, Latina Style, Minority Business News,* and *Black Enterprise* magazine. In 2004, for the 10th year in a row, Nordstrom partnered with *Hispanic Business* to recognize the publication's Teacher of the Year. In its mainstream advertising, Nordstrom has long been committed to featuring models of color and models with disabilities in at least one-third of its advertisements.

Another way Nordstrom attracts minority employees is to invest in minority projects. In 1989, Nordstrom created a Minority- and Women-Owned Supplier Diversity Program. When Nordstrom enters a new market, the company sets out to cultivate minority-owned and women-owned vendors of office supplies, food, music, photography, and other services, including construction. Through its Supplier Diversity Program, the company also encourages women- and minority-owned businesses to supply locally produced merchandise. Thanks to the company's decentralized buying, Nordstrom is able to bring in smaller vendors and try out their products.

Today, Nordstrom annually spends almost $600 million with minority and/or women-owned vendors.

"What makes this thing work is that it is such a diverse group of people, with all these different experiences," said Blake Nordstrom. "I believe we are the sum of our experiences. How do you hire people with those elements and also get different points of view? That's the challenge. We have to be reflective of our communities and our customer base. We need to encourage different styles and points of view."

Blake and his father, Bruce, both point out that about half of the Nordstrom employees that reach sales of one million dollars or more are of foreign extraction. "These people remind my dad of his grandfather [founder John W.] who came to this country from nothing and could barely speak English," noted Blake.

Although all of these top salespeople arrived in the United States with far greater academic credentials than John W., they do share his entrepreneurial spirit.

For example, Van Mensah, the men's suit salesman at the Pentagon City, Virginia, store outside of Washington, DC, is a native of Ghana, who holds an MBA degree from Northeastern University in Boston.

In the late 1980s, Mensah was a department manager for home furnishings, fine china, and furniture at the Woodward & Lothrop department store in Washington, DC. At that time, Woodward & Lothrop was anxiously preparing for the arrival of its new competitor, Nordstrom, which was opening its first East Coast store at Tysons Corner. Woodward & Lothrop tried to get its employees to act more like Nordstrom employees by showing an instructional video on how Nordstrom operated, and how it empowered employees to make decisions.

"That was the first time I had heard about Nordstrom," recalled Mensah. "I thought, 'This would be a nice company to work for,'" He soon left Woodward & Lothrop and joined Nordstrom in 1988, as a member of the original staff at Tysons Corner.

For the past 12 years, as a men's suit salesman, Mensah has been a Pacesetter every year, and a million-dollar seller for many years. As for Woodward & Lothrop, it went out of business in 1996.

Nader Shafii, a native of Tehran, Iran, came to the United States in 1975, and six years later graduated from Eastern Oregon State University. Soon after, he moved to Portland, Oregon, where he went to work part-time at Nordstrom's Washington Square store. At the time, he was not considering a career in retail. He was still searching for what he wanted to do with his life.

"On several occasions, I met members of the Nordstrom family at store meetings," he recalls. John, Bruce, and Jim Nordstrom (the group who ran the company from the late 1960s to the mid-1990s), would often "walk around the store and talk to the people on the floor. As a business graduate, I was impressed that the co-presidents of the company would talk to the sales staff on the floor and ask questions. It intrigued me. I felt the warmth, the closeness among the managers and staff. You did not feel it was a boss/subordinate relationship. That's when I started to look more seriously at a career in retail. The more I listened to them speak, the more I understood what this company is based on. It changed me from wanting to have a job to having a career. I stayed in retail, specifically at Nordstrom, because of who these people were."

Today, Shafii works in the Personal Touch department at the store in the South Coast Plaza, in Costa Mesa, California. In Chapter 10, we will explore how he runs his business within the Nordstrom structure.

The Nordies versus the Clock Punchers

Despite its strong reputation as an employer, Nordstrom has had problems with certain members of its workforce.

In 1990, Nordstrom found itself in a battle with the union that represented the five original stores in the company's home area of Seattle and Tacoma—the only stores in the chain that were represented by a union. Many veteran employees wanted to make union membership optional; the union was solidly opposed to that proposition and fought it when the contract was up for renewal.

The union engaged in a highly publicized public relations campaign in an effort to harm the company. It never called a strike because it did not have the votes of the rank and file.

The union charged that Nordstrom was not paying employees for hand-delivering purchases to customers at their homes or places of business, and was not compensating employees for doing inventory and other tasks.

Ultimately, Nordstrom set up a claims process to deal with complaints of off-the-clock work. Pay practices were changed and a new policy was laid out for employees to record all hours worked. Nordstrom immediately began paying workers for attending store meetings, doing inventory work, and making "hand carries"—picking up merchandise at one store and delivering it to another. If done during regular work hours, hand carries would be covered as part of an employee's selling hours, which determine sales-per-hour performance. Recording this additional hour was a disincentive for top salespeople because vacation pay was determined by sales-per-hour results. Other deliveries that were made to help the department would be considered "non-sell" hours, and would not affect sales-per-hour performance. (Employees would receive an hourly wage for that time.) When making deliveries going to or from work, pay would be calculated over and above the regular commute time. The same criteria would apply to a salesperson's delivery to a customer's home, office, or hotel. The Nordstrom rulebook was expanded, at least metaphorically, by a few pages.

Many enterprising salespeople disagreed in principle with being paid specifically for deliveries made to their personal customers. "Customer service means being there when the customer needs you," said salesperson Annette Carmony. "I sometimes deliver things to a customer who is disabled. That's part of my job. Our structure gives us more flexibility with the customer, and the payoff is always going to be there. Without my personals, I wouldn't be making the money I do." On one typical day, before her shift began, Carmony drove to another Portland-area Nordstrom to pick up a dress for a customer who had to attend a funeral, and then drove back to the Washington Square store where she handed over the garment to the deeply appreciative customer. Later that day, Carmony delivered another dress to a customer who needed it by a certain time but couldn't get to the store. Those kinds of heroics "make Nordstrom look even better in the customer's eyes."

The people who do the best for the company (and themselves) are the ones who respond to the system, work the hardest, and do the extra things that it takes to be more productive. "I can't fault those people who say [doing extra tasks] is part of their job and that they need to get paid for them," said Joe Dover, who at the time was a veteran shoe salesman and an opponent of the Union. "But there still has to be room to allow salespersons to be the best they can be, to take the initiative to do the extra things. What's wrong with writing thank-you notes at home on your own time, or getting the walls stocked to make your area easier to sell in? It will make your income better. I do get paid for that type of work; my commissions prove it. It's ludicrous to be forced to pay someone to sit down and write a thank-you note. How do you make someone be nice to a customer?"[1]

[1] On January 11, 1993, the UFCW's class action lawsuit ended in an out-of-court settlement. Current and former Nordstrom employees who worked at least 200 regular hours between February 16, 1987, and March 15, 1990, were eligible to file claims for off-the-clock wage compensation. Commissioned sales personnel received three hours pay for every 100 hours worked during the period for a total of up to $2,000. Noncommissioned personnel received 1.2 hours pay for every 100 hours worked. Overtime wages were paid to eligible class members employed during the period from February 16, 1987, to September 15, 1992. The total outlay was for considerably less than Peterson's most conservative estimate. Nordstrom paid out approximately $5 million under the settlement, with a median payout of $170. Only 1,444 people received checks for more than $1,000. Several people received about $7,000. All of them had worked in one department in one state, where the method of calculating overtime had been done incorrectly, not only by Nordstrom, but other stores as well. About 1,900 checks were for less than $10.00.

The big pay off went to the union's attorneys: legal fees and costs of administering the settlement came to about $6.6 million.

Hiring Your Own Nordstrom-Quality Employees _____

The Number One thing people ask Robert Spector when he speaks to corporate groups is "Where can I find good young people who respond to customers with the words 'thank you' or 'you're welcome' or 'my pleasure,' rather than 'sorry, we don't do that.'"

You can teach new people the nuts and bolts, the mechanics of the job, the technical aspects, but you can't teach them to be nice.

W Hotel attracts people who would like to become actors or models, which is why employees are called "cast members." Job interviews are appropriately labeled "casting calls," and the jobs are described as roles to be played—not on a proscenium stage, but rather a hotel lobby, restaurant, or registration desk.

When it identifies a new market, the hotel dispatches an army of recruiters that comb the city and scout potential employees. "If we get tremendous service in a place, we let that person know who we are, how impressed we are," said Tom Limberg, general manager of the W Hotel in Seattle.

Nordstrom does the same thing in seeking out potential new employees.

St. Charles Medical Center in Bend, Oregon, draws its staff from three counties—Deschuttes, Crook, and Jefferson—covering about 25,000 square miles and a population of 150,000. With that small a pool of qualified people to choose from, recruiting becomes particularly crucial at an institution that doesn't leverage its most valuable asset, its employees, according to chief executive officer emeritus Jim Lussier.

In a preapplication process, St. Charles cuts to the quick: "What's your mission in life? Why are you in health care? Why do you want to work at St. Charles? Does their aspiration for how they want to perform in their profession match what we need in an employee? We try to make clear to any new applicant that this is a different environment from what you would find normally," said Lussier. "We are certainly interested in your clinical skills, but you have to bring those other people skills and the ability to work in a team setting, as well as be motivated by all the right things to be able to work at St. Charles."

Applicants are also interviewed by members of the team in which they are going to work, so the team members have a say in whether that new person will fit in.

"The environment in which we place patients is largely determined by the human staff that we have, and it is augmented by the physical environment. But it's the human staff that's the real turnkey," said Lussier. "In health care, we used to hire anybody who was a warm body. If you had an RN degree or were a good lab technician or whatever and could carry out clinical work, that's who we hired. Today, we're saying: 'That's not it. We can virtually teach anybody the technical skills. It's the motivational stuff. It's being able to be an adult, handle your own conflicts, work in a team setting.'"

Realty Executives of Las Vegas: Ask Lots of Questions

At Realty Executives, all the people hired are experienced agents, who are independent contractors. Agents, who earn their money through sales commissions, pay Realty Executives a fixed management fee of $395 per month and a fixed transaction fee of $395 per closing, which covers a variety of services, including continuing education, broker support, broker management; attorney services, and the rent on the office building.

These independent contractors must uphold their own reputation, as well as that of Realty Executives.

Consequently, "We are going to ask a lot of questions in the interview about their source of business, and their professionalism and ethics," said Fafie Moore, co-owner of the firm, who has found that, "our reputation has helped our recruiting."

"I'll ask, 'What are you looking for in a company? What are you looking for in a manager?'" said Moore "After I have a feel for what you're looking for, I'm going to explain to you how Realty Executives is going to help meet those needs for you. If you say things that tell me that you don't have the same [ethical] guidance system that we do, I'm probably going to suggest that this is not the place for you, because that's not the way we do things."

Jeff Moore, Fafie's husband and partner, emphasized how important it is for agents who work together to like each other. "The attitude of the individual is just as important as their skill level," he said. "You can teach somebody the mechanics of being a salesperson, but you can't change the attitude."

Mike's Express Carwash

Because of the labor and hiring laws, an employer has to be extremely careful as to the kind of questions he asks potential employees in interview situations.

"I like to ask open-ended questions," said Mike Dahm of Mike's Express Carwash. "For example, I'll ask, 'Will you share with me whatever you're comfortable sharing, so that I can get to know you better as a person?' Generally, applicants will talk about their family, their school; things like that."

"We try to find out as much as we can about how applicants feel about themselves. And how they feel about waiting on customers. Some people are cut out for service and some people aren't."

At a brainstorming session that Robert Spector conducted with one of his clients, a builder of residential urban housing, company employees came up with the following ideas when it came to hiring:

- Allow department members to meet with prospective employees before hiring.
- When you notice someone with a great personality/work ethic in another field or industry, offer them a business card and an opportunity to come speak with us.
- Be committed to hiring the best—don't just hire someone because we need the position filled.
- Bring people in from internships, expand summer intern opportunities.
- By following these simple keys, you can find the people who will make yours a great customer service company.

Nordstrom knows what it wants in an employee. Does your organization know what it wants in an employee? Only by understanding your organization, its requirements, and its culture can your organization become the Nordstrom of your industry.

Keys to Success

What do you look for in an employee—a warm body or someone who can take over when you're not around? Is previous experience in your industry a requirement? Or are you like Nordstrom, where you would rather hire someone who is friendly, someone who is inspired to do a great job just because that's the way that person was raised? Every great customer service company is looking for nice, motivated, energetic, entrepreneurial people, who are the building blocks that go into creating a company where customer service is paramount.

- Previous industry experience should not be the determining factor.

- Hire people who enjoy people and who are excited about the job.

- Hire the smile, train the skill.

- Hire the personality and the confidence.

- Hire people who share your values.

- Involve potential coworkers or team members in the interview and hiring process.

- Treat employees with dignity and respect.

- Invest in the people who are cut out for service.

EXERCISE

Hiring Questionnaire

How do you find people who are service- and results-oriented and are also team players? First of all, you need to ask them the right questions when you are interviewing them.

- Assemble a broad cross-section of your long-time employees in one room.

- Select a person to lead the discussion.

- Compile a list of questions that elicit the following attributes in new hires:

  1. A sense of customer service.
  2. A definition of customer service.
  3. A desire to give customer service.
  4. A willingness to work hard.
  5. Self-motivation.
  6. Independence.
  7. Judgment.
  8. Creativity.
  9. Dealing with difficult customers.
  10. Teamwork.
  11. An ability to achieve results.
  12. A competitive spirit.

- Distribute this list to the rest of your company.

- Organize the list and make it a formal element for hiring in your organization.

6

That's My Job

Empower Employees to Act Like Entrepreneurs to Satisfy the Customer

Entrepreneurs are simply those who understand that there is little difference between obstacle and opportunity and are able to turn both to their advantage.

—Niccolo Machiavelli

If you boil the Nordstrom system down to its essence, down to the one sentence that separates Nordstrom from most other companies it is this: *Nordstrom gives its people on the sales floor the freedom to make entrepreneurial decisions, and management backs them on those decisions.* Everything else flows from that simple premise.

That's called *empowerment.* In most businesses, it's a cliché. At Nordstrom, it's a vital reality.

At most companies and organizations, the hard part for an employer and a manager is having the courage to empower employees to take ownership. That's what Nordstrom does so well.

The Nordstrom system is entrepreneurial. Everett, Elmer, and Lloyd Nordstrom, who bought the business from their father, John W., in the late 1920s, knew that the best way to attract and retain motivated, self-starters was to pay them according to their ability. Ever since the early 1950s, when Nordstrom was selling only shoes, employee compensation has been based on commissions on net sales.

Commission sales and bonuses "gave them added incentive to work harder, and by working harder, they were often able to build a loyal customer following," Elmer Nordstrom wrote in *A Winning Team,* the privately published family history.

To maintain that loyal customer following, Nordstrom allows salespeople to sell merchandise to their customers in any department throughout the store. The company believes that once a salesperson has established rapport with a customer and has helped that customer put together the right look, the salesperson wants to make sure all of the customer's needs are met in order to complete the package.

For example, let's say you are buying a suit in the men's wear department. Then you realize you need some shirts and underwear; your suit salesman can sell those items to you, even though they are in a different department. That salesman could even sell you a sweater for your wife or a skirt for your daughter.

The freedom to sell throughout the store gives go-go salespeople greater opportunity for higher sales. A now-retired top Nordstrom saleswoman once described her business as "one-stop shopping. If it's not nailed down, I'll find it for the customer. A customer once wanted a case of hangers, so I ordered them from our distribution center. Another customer wanted to buy some of our long, plastic garment bags. I didn't make commission on those things, but it's part of the service I provided."

Commission Structure

Commission sales are a prime reason why Nordstrom salespeople embrace the empowerment that the company affords them.

The standard commission at Nordstrom is 6.75 percent on apparel sales. Other commission rates vary according to product category.

Each salesperson has a designated draw, which is determined by dividing the hourly rate by a commission percentage. That rate varies, depending on the competitive rates in each region. (At Nordstrom, the top range is from $9.00 to $11.25 per hour.) The amount of the draw varies with each department. In men's sportswear, for example, the 6.75 percent commission rate divided into an hourly wage rate of $11.25 equals $166.66 in sales per hour, which is Nordstrom's minimum hourly sales target for that specific department. At the end of each pay period, sales-per-hour performance is calculated by taking the gross dollar volume of items sold, subtracting returns, and dividing that figure by the number of hours worked. For example, a salesperson rings up $22,000 in sales in an 80-hour pay period. Subtract $2,000 for returns, and the net total sales are $20,000, or $250 per hour. That salesperson's commission for the pay period is 6.75 percent of $20,000, or $1,350.

Many top Nordstrom salespeople have said that if they were being paid only an hourly rate, they wouldn't be as motivated as they are. Knowing that their commission reflects how hard they work instills a different kind of drive. Nordstrom allows salespeople to grow based on what they produce.

Because it constantly stresses the importance of sales, Nordstrom promotes a dynamic tension among its employees. All of them have ready access to sales figures from all departments and stores in the Nordstrom chain, so they can compare their performance with that of their colleagues—whether those colleagues work across the selling floor or across the country.

One of the most important performance barometers is sales-per-hour, or "SPH," in the Nordstrom mother tongue. Each employee's semi-monthly sales-per-hour figures are posted clearly in a backroom of the store for everyone in the department to see. So you know how I'm doing and I know how you're doing. Needless to say, the bottom of the standings is not where you want to be.

The top-performing salespeople at Nordstrom are designated "Pacesetters," which means that they meet or surpass the goal for net-sales-volume (sales minus returns and held returns) for their specific department for the one-year period from December 16 through December 15 of the following year.

Becoming a Pacesetter takes dedication, hard work, and a feeling of ownership of their own business, which comes about through empowerment.

Pacesetters are given a certificate of merit, an event, or an outing in their honor, business cards emblazoned with the Pacesetter designation, and a 33 percent merchandise discount credit card (13 percent more than the regular employee discount) for one year.

"When you have star salespeople, they ought to get paid like stars because they earn it," said Bruce Nordstrom.

If salespeople aren't making enough in commissions to cover their draw, then Nordstrom makes up the difference between commissions earned and their hourly rate. Employees who fail to regularly exceed their draw are targeted for special coaching by their department manager. If it doesn't appear that a career in sales is for them, they are either assigned to a nonsales area or are let go.

(A more detailed explanation of Pacesetter designation as well as other sales honors will be discussed in greater detail in Chapter 9.)

Empower Employees to Make Good Decisions

Even as it grows, Nordstrom strives "to put as much responsibility as possible into the hands of as many people as possible," said Bruce Nordstrom. "That's the only way to give the culture a chance to progress. Otherwise, it can't be done. With almost 50,000 employees, spread out over 3,000 miles, if you were dependent on a Nordstrom family member, you couldn't do it. We keep pushing the power down to the sales floor. Human nature being what it is, there's no question that if you are in an ivory tower, sitting at a desk behind your computer and your reports, you'll say, 'I'm scared of the decisions they're going to make down on the floor.'

"I sometimes sit in my office here and wring my hands, but I know that in the long run, [our way] is better. I think I'm a good shoe man. I think with a little crash course, I could be a good shoe buyer today. But there's no way I should be telling these folks what colors to buy, what heel heights to buy, what patterns to buy because I don't know enough about it. I'm not talking to those customers every day. If that confidence in the individual is repeated over and over and over again, it creates power there. This isn't a real scientific business. If we could harness people's good will, energy, and ideas and have it all go in one direction, then it would have to be successful."

Nordstrom has confidence in its salespeople's ability to make good choices. If the store manager or department manager isn't around to approve a key decision, the salesperson can make the decision—even if it's wrong.

Len Kuntz, vice president of the Washington/Alaska region, said that when he was a store manager, whenever a salesperson asked him for advice on how to accommodate a customer's request, he would turn the question around and ask what the salesperson thought. "I'm not smarter than anybody else. So many things are common sense," said Kuntz. "This business is much simpler than people make it out to be. If you give people leeway and credit, most of the time they're going to do the right thing. It's just like when you are a child: You imitate what you see. If you see a great example, you're going to imitate that."

But some people can't handle that freedom. John Whitacre (the late former chairman of Nordstrom), who in 1988 oversaw the opening of Nordstrom's first East Coast store at Tysons Corner Center in McLean, Virginia, used to tell the story of one training session prior to the opening of the store. A new sales-person admitted that she would have difficulty functioning in such a freewheeling atmosphere. "Tell me exactly what you want me to do," she told Whitacre, "and I promise I'll do it that way." But Nordstrom's freedom attracts "people who give a damn," Whitacre told Robert Spector. "We want to reward people who don't require a lot of supervision, who see this as a place to do their thing, within parameters. That's the way our pay, bonus, and profit-sharing systems are set up."

One of the new East Coast employees who immediately grasped the Nordstrom Way was Van Mensah (whom we visited in Chapter 5), the men's apparel salesperson at Nordstrom's Pentagon City, Virginia, store. Mensah, who joined the company in 1988, has an extensive international clientele of gentlemen whose jobs bring them to the nation's capital. His 2,800 active customers include many international business people, government officials—particularly in the diplomatic community—as well as U.S. senators, congressmen, and military officials.

Whenever he's not selling to a customer in the store, Mensah is on the phone, and he routinely makes 25 to 30 customer calls per day.

"This is where the whole philosophy of empowerment makes so much sense," he said. "You are empowered to use your own time wisely."

One day, Mensah received a disturbing letter from one of his better customers, an executive with a well-known Swedish-based manufacturer. The gentleman had recently purchased some $2,000 worth of shirts and ties from Mensah, and when he mistakenly washed the shirts in hot water, they all shrank. He was not writing to complain (he readily conceded the mistake was his), but to ask Mensah's professional advice on how he should deal with his predicament.

Mensah immediately put a telephone call through to Sweden and told the customer that he would replace those shirts with new ones at no charge. He asked the customer to mail the other shirts back to Nordstrom—at Nordstrom's expense.

This story was written up in a Nordstrom annual report to shareholders entitled "A Company of Entrepreneurs." So, here is a publicly-traded corporation telling its shareholders that they have this employee who gave away $2,000 worth of merchandise—and that they are so proud of him, they are featuring him in the annual report.

"I didn't have to ask for anyone's permission to do what I did for that customer," said Mensah, a native of Ghana, who holds an MBA degree from Northeastern University in Boston. "Nordstrom would rather leave it up to me to decide what's best."

Most companies can't afford to give away $2,000 worth of goods. In this case it was a good business decision because of the loyalty it bred in a valuable customer. But don't be diverted by that grand gesture. Great customer service doesn't have to be the grand gesture. It can be just as powerful when it's a small gesture, a human kindness. Robert Spector experienced that at a Starbucks Coffee store in his neighborhood of West Seattle. Spector was there to buy a pound of Arabian Mocha Java beans. He brought in his empty one-pound bag because Starbucks takes 10 cents off the price when a customer brings in a used bag for a refill. Spector handed his bag to the young woman behind the counter, who looked at it and said, "Your bag is pretty worn out. I'll give you a new bag, but I'll still take 10 cents off the price." For a brief moment, that gesture made him feel good. Ten cents off the price. Of course, he was paying 14 dollars for that pound of coffee, but the bottom line is that the employee's small gesture created a positive feeling toward Starbucks.

Return Policy

Empowering the people on the sales floor with the freedom to accept returned merchandise (even when the damage was done by the customer) is the most noticeable illustration of the Nordstrom culture because it is the one that most obviously affects the public.

Nordstrom's return policy is virtually an unconditional, money-back guarantee. (There are some exceptions, due to public health laws, in certain departments, such as cosmetics.) If customers aren't completely satisfied with their purchase, for whatever reason, the store takes it back, no questions asked. Chairman Bruce Nordstrom tells salespeople, "If a customer came into the store with a pair of five-year-old shoes and complained that the shoes were worn out and wanted her money back, you have the right to use your best judgment to give the customer her money back."

This is not hyperbole. In 2000, an item in the *Seattle Times* told the story of a couple of Seattle women who were packing the belongings of one of the women who was moving. They discovered two pairs of long-forgotten dress shoes that were never worn, still in their original boxes with Nordstrom price tags and a sales slip—from 1987. Half-joking, the women returned the shoes to Nordstrom, which reimbursed them the original price of the shoes, a total of $98.50.

Doesn't that unconditional policy invite abuse? Sure it does, but central to the Nordstrom philosophy is a desire not to punish the many for the dishonesty of a few.

Which is not to say that returns are not often frustrating for Nordstrom salespeople. You have that customer who "borrows" a dress for a couple of years and then returns it. But top salespeople realize that returns are part of the game; they take back the returns with a smile, knowing that many of those customers will come back.

Some enterprising Nordstrom salespeople will even send a thank-you note to a customer who has returned a purchase. Wouldn't a gesture like that get your attention as a customer?

That kind of resourceful thinking was exactly what Everett, Elmer, and Lloyd Nordstrom had in mind when they established this generous warranty back when Nordstrom was a two-store operation. The brothers dreaded having to deal with obviously outrageous or unreasonable returns, so, they reckoned, if they could pass off the responsibilities for the adjustments and complaints, the business would be more personally enjoyable.

"We decided to let the clerks make the adjustments, so they would be the fair-haired boys," recalled Elmer. "We told them, 'If the customer is not pleased, she can come to us and we'll give her what she wants anyway.'" The Nordstroms tracked the costs of the return policy for the first year and found they could afford to maintain it. Plus, in a world where most retailers made returns an ordeal, Nordstrom made the experience as painless as possible, which generated priceless word-of-mouth advertising. It still does.

Perhaps the most famous Nordstrom return story—which the national press frequently cites—is the tale of the salesperson who gladly took back a set of automobile tires and gave the customer a refund. What's wrong with this story? Nordstrom has never sold tires, but the story is true. In 1975, Nordstrom acquired three stores in Alaska, from the Northern Commercial Company, which was a full-line department store that sold many products, including tires. After Nordstrom bought the stores, the company converted them to Nordstrom, eliminated lots of departments, including the tire department. So, when the customer—who purchased the tires from Northern Commercial (not Nordstrom)—brought them back to Nordstrom, the return was accepted. This has become the quintessential Nordstrom return story, and Robert Spector hears variations of it wherever he travels.

Inverted Pyramid

Nordstrom's empowerment culture is illustrated by the company's informal structure of an inverted pyramid (see Figure 6.1). At the very top of the pyramid are the customers, and beneath

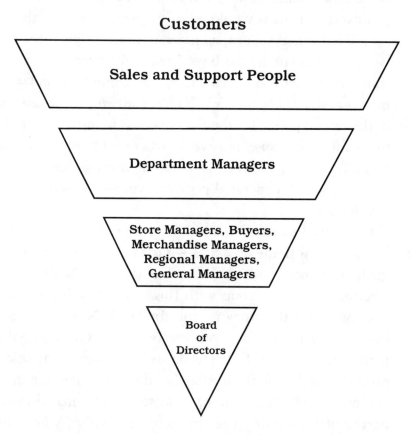

Figure 6.1 Nordstrom's inverted organizational pyramid.

them are the salespeople, department managers, and executives, all the way down to the board of directors. This is both a literal and symbolic way of how the company does its business. The customers are obviously on top because they are the most important people in the equation. But the *next* most important are the salespeople because they are the ones who are closest to the customers. And it is the job of the rest of the people in the organization to help those people on the sales floor—the front lines—because they are the engine that powers the machine. If *they* aren't making money, then the company isn't making money.

The inverted pyramid was born in the early 1970s, when Nordstrom made its initial public offering of stock. A stock analyst asked the company for its organizational chart. To his surprise, none existed. Somebody suggested that "we take a pyramid and flip it upside down," recalled John N. Nordstrom. What sets Nordstrom apart is that, from department manager to chairman, all tiers of the inverted pyramid work to support the sales staff, not the other way around. "The only thing we have going for us is the way we take care of our customers," explained Ray Johnson, retired co-chairman, "and the people who take care of the customers are on the floor."

Nordstrom has many ways to get feedback from the people on the sales floor. For example, every year, the company flies in to Seattle all the salespeople who have recorded a million dollars or more in sales.

"We are closest to the market," said Van Mensah, one of those million-dollar performers. "We talk about different trends. What we need to do to improve the business. A lot of things we talk about get implemented. We give that advice freely." The company saves a lot of money by getting advice from people inside the company rather than bringing in a consultant who has no clue on how to sell to a customer. Our markets are different. By bringing in all these people from different markets, you get a good idea of your total business.

Nader Shafii, a million-dollar salesman in the South Coast Plaza store in Orange County, California, recollected in particular a meeting where then-co-chairman Jim Nordstrom (who passed away in 1996) addressed buyers and managers and some Pacesetters.

"Mr. Jim told the buyers and managers that the salespeople on the floor were the most important people in the company because they are the people between management and the customers," recalled Nader. "He said, 'The salespeople are the ones who can bring the message from the customers to management—they tell us what they need in order to be able to make the customers happy. If the salespeople are not happy with the product, the buyers and managers should know. You should be able to react to that.' To me, that was a huge statement. That was the turning point for me."

Like all top Nordstrom salespeople, Shafii feels that he is running his own business, with the support of every level of management.

"If you are willing to go above and beyond the call of duty, Nordstrom is 100 percent behind you," said Shafii. "You have all the support and all the tools. It's up to you to see where you would like to go with it."

The freedom and support inherent in a Nordstrom culture that encourages ownership and entrepreneurship is symbolized by the inverted pyramid. Individual frontline Nordstrom salespeople essentially run their own business within the larger corporate structure. At Nordstrom, it is obvious that the salespeople are the most important elements in the organization; management supports those people every step of the way. The Nordstrom system enables and encourages each salesperson to use his or her own personality and approach and skills to succeed. Therefore, individuals can put their own stamp on how they do business.

In a Nordstrom employee newspaper, salespeople were asked the question: "What Does the Inverted Pyramid Mean to Me?"

Xochitl Flores, an employee at one of the Nordstrom Rack (clearance) stores in Northern California, recalled the time when her store was closing up for the night and all of the cash registers were shut down. Before she left, Flores noticed one credit card payment had accidentally gone unprocessed. "When I saw that the payment was due that night, I drove it over to our Stonestown store, which was still open, so I could make sure the customer wouldn't receive a finance charge. Because my manager believes in me, I believe in myself and feel confident to take on more responsibility instead of doing the same job and the same tasks every day."

What I like about the story is that Xochitl prevented something from happening, which the customer never realized. Let's say Xochitl had decided, "Oh, why bother. It's not my problem. Somebody will process the bill tomorrow." Then imagine you were that customer. You get your bill from Nordstrom and you notice that there is a late charge. You think to yourself, "Not only did I pay that bill on time, I paid it right in the store. How did Nordstrom screw this up?" Instantly, this customer has a negative feeling about Nordstrom. But that didn't happen because one empowered employee, inspired by her employer's (and her coworkers') commitment to customer service, drove miles out of her way to save that customer a late charge. At Nordstrom, small gestures count as much as grand gestures.

Empowering Buyers and Managers _____

Back in the mid-twentieth century, when making buying decisions at the New York wholesale shoe markets, Everett Nordstrom encouraged young buyers to develop their own ideas and make their own decisions. Everett's brother Elmer used to tell the story of what happened when one shoe manufacturer's sales staff showed their line to both Everett and a young buyer of women's shoes (the store's biggest department), and then turned to Everett for his reaction. "Don't talk to me," said Everett, "this is my buyer." The sales representatives then turned their eyes toward the nervous 22-year-old buyer. "After that, the fellow worked his heart out for the company," Elmer recalled.

Like everyone else at Nordstrom, department managers begin their careers as salespeople in order to learn what's required to take care of the customer.

You start at the bottom and do it the Nordstrom way, and those standards are nonnegotiable.

Current company president Blake Nordstrom—like his brothers, Pete and Erik—first began working in the store at the age of 10, sweeping floors in the downtown shoe stockroom. At 13, he stocked shoes; at 15, he began selling shoes and from then on, worked while attending the University of Washington, and after graduation as a buyer, merchandiser, department manager and store manager in company stores around the country.

"Because we have a promote-from-within culture, in this company you don't graduate from college and go to the corner office," said Erik Nordstrom, executive vice president of full-line stores. Growing up, "the vast majority of my cousins worked at the store at one point or another. It was a very natural thing to come to the store after school to sell shoes or work at some similar level. Some of my cousins eventually decided to do other things. For me, I stuck with it because I liked it."

Erik felt it was a natural progression for him and his brothers to start working in stock and then moving "to co-third assistant in women's shoes to a second assistant," and so on long before ever taking on any management responsibilities. "We were all well served by that."

Pete Nordstrom, executive vice president of the company, and president of its full-line stores division, "can't imagine doing my job, or any job I've ever had in this company, without being grounded in how it all plays out at the point of sale. The moment of truth is what happens between salespeople and customers. So, every decision we make—based on every experience we have had—must go back to supporting the relationship between the salespeople and the customers. For example, I would be of no help to a salesperson who has a question about returning a suit if I hadn't done that exact same thing a few times myself."

"Starting on the sales floor sends the signal from management that it values that role more than almost anything. All up and down the organization, people appreciate the importance of this function and what it means for everything else in the organization. It's critical," said Alfred E. Osborne Jr., a Nordstrom director. The Nordstrom family's own sales experiences fostered an appreciation for what salespeople go through and what it takes to satisfy customers. As they readily concede, when they were young salespeople and didn't have what the customer asked for, they weren't good enough salespeople to be able to switch the customer to another item.

Managers are encouraged to have a feeling of ownership about their department. They are responsible for hiring (the Human Resources department does little recruitment), firing,

scheduling, training, coaching, nurturing, encouraging, and evaluating their sales team. Rather than sit behind a desk, Nordstrom
managers, like the proprietors of small boutiques, are expected to
spend some of their time on the selling floor, interacting with
the customers and the sales staff. They are paid a salary plus commission on any sales they make, and are eligible for a bonus tied
to percentage increases in sales over the previous year.

Kimiko Gubbins, a Nordstrom women's sportswear buyer for
its Rack discount division, appreciated that Nordstrom allows its
buyers the freedom "to help create and shape a department and
gives us the full authority to do what we need to do to make a
business exist."

Nordstrom buyers have to be just as aware of customer service as its salespeople.

"My customer service is to my managers and salespeople because they are talking to the customers," says Kimiko. "I need
their feedback to help shape my buy."

Len Kuntz said, "It doesn't matter what the department manager does as much as what everybody else is doing." The Nordstrom executive characterized the role of department manager
as "probably the hardest job in our company. You have to have a
lot of balls in the air." Yet department manager has been his favorite post at Nordstrom because "you can teach people and
build strong teams. The only difference between stores is the
people they have."

The store manager's primary responsibility is to set the tone
for what happens on the sales floor. "I spent 75 percent of my
time on the sales floor interacting with the managers, the salespeople, and the customers," said Kuntz. "When customers looked
lost, I offered them directions. When your people see you doing
that, they realize that's the focus of the company. Much of what

happens in this company is environmental. You absorb it by watching and seeing the focus and priorities, and it snowballs."

By empowering salespeople and managers at all levels a wide range of operational and bottom-line responsibility (such as controlling costs), without shackling them with lots of bureaucratic guidelines that get in the way of serving the customer, Nordstrom allows its people to operate like entrepreneurial shopkeepers rather than blocks in a retailing monolith.

Buyers get their feedback directly from the salespeople and the customers because they are encouraged to spend several hours a week on the sales floor. "Interacting with the customer is so powerful," said Len Kuntz. "Computer spreadsheets can tell you what's selling, but they can't tell you what you're not selling because you don't have it in stock. The best buyers in our company are good listeners." Customers appreciate being able to talk directly with a manager or a buyer. If a customer wants to know when a particular shoe will be in stock, a salesperson can turn to her buyer or manager and get the answer immediately.

Implementation Lessons from Other Companies

A core value at FirstMerit bank is that individual employees are empowered to make a difference in the customer's life. "Everyone of our people is trained to take control of any customer situation they face. There's nothing that they can't handle," said chairman and CEO John Cochran. "We tell them that they can make a difference in the life of the customer they are servicing at this moment.

"Our goal is to empower the FirstMerit team members—whether a receptionist, a teller, a call center employee, a services division employee, front-line banker, or CEO—so that they can serve the customer with a blend of urgency and enthusiasm."

One of the credos at the bank is the phrase *I make a difference*. "We understand that our competitive advantage is in the hands of each individual and only when those hands are part of the team do they provide an unmatched experience for our customers," said Cochran.

"Like Nordstrom, we ask our people to use their common sense," added Cochran. "We want them to ask themselves what action can they take that will fundamentally be best for the customer. It goes back to empowering your people to take ownership of the customer situation. For example, if you have to waive a charge on the spot, you do it. If you have to make an apology for the institution, you do it."

Like every great customer-service organization, the nonprofit organization Feed the Children "wants to push the decision-making responsibility and authority down to the lowest level possible," said vice president Paul Bigham. "Our charge to the people who work for Feed the Children is this: 'You can do anything you want as long as you stay within certain parameters. Don't go out of those parameters. Inside, those parameters, I don't want to hear from you. If you don't feel comfortable in making the call, go up-line and let someone else make the call."

In 1995, when terrorists bombed the Alfred P. Murrah Building in Oklahoma City, Feed the Children's hometown, the employees of the charity sprang into action. Director Larry Jones sent out the word to local officials: "If I've got it, you can have it. If I don't have it, I'll find it. If I can't find it, we'll buy it." As Bigham recalled, "That was our mantra for the next few weeks as people worked around that clock."

In the aftermath of the bombing, harried rescue workers spent days removing blocks of concrete, digging through the rubble in a Herculean effort to locate survivors. Those who were there remember it as a surreal scene of debris and destruction, accompanied by the constant humming of generators, which supplied the power to illuminate the building. In the middle of all of that, a sleet storm swept through the scene. Through it all, courageous men and women continued to work in the bitter cold, 12 and 14 hours at a stretch, pulling out dead bodies and parts of dead bodies. When they found they needed metal kneepads to protect them from the shrapnel, Feed the Children located the kneepads, and arranged with American Airlines to fly them to Oklahoma City.

"When they took their breaks, the men asked for two things: warm socks and cigars," said Bigham. "Somehow, one of our employees took it upon himself to locate some Tiparillos. I don't remember where we found them, but I delivered them. I'll never forget those guys coming back from this horrid, horrible, grotesque place; this den of death, and just sort of connect to reality again. We couldn't have been able to do that without a Feed the Children worker empowered to do whatever the job required."

"We tell our employees: do whatever it takes to make a customer happy," said Bill Dahm, president of Mike's Express Carwash. "The guy who started on the job yesterday has just as much authority as a 10-year veteran employee to walk up to a customer and say, 'We're not happy with the wash. We want to give you a rewash. Would you mind going through again?'"

As a vehicle to reward and recognize outstanding customer service by employees, Mike's initiated what the company calls its WOW Program. Every time the company receives a letter or an e-mail praising one of the associates for performing a customer service act above and beyond the call of duty, that associate is given a "WOW" pin, and is rewarded financially, and later with a plaque at the company's annual awards banquet. By emphasizing the WOW experience, and repeatedly telling employees that they are empowered to do whatever it takes to make the customer happy, Mike's has created a culture of empowered employees.

A WOW moment could be something as simple as fixing the flat tire of a noncustomer who was stranded near a Mike's Carwash or driving home a customer who accidentally locked his keys in his car. And it could be something as dramatic as saving a choking child by performing the Heimlich Maneuver.

"You're not really there to do those things, but you do whatever it takes to make customers happy so they want to keep coming back," said Dahm.

Great customer service companies give their people the power to make the situation right—right away.

One Friday afternoon, an elderly couple brought their car in to Mike's before leaving town to visit their son in Michigan. They bought "The Works"—Mike's ultimate service of washing and shining—in preparation for the special weekend. After taking their car through the wash, the couple came back around and parked in front of Mike's building. When they got out of their car, manager Monte Montgomery came up to greet them, saw immediately that the woman was obviously upset. She told him that while sitting in her car as it went through the automated wash, the high pressure rinse was too strong, water squirted through her window, and she had gotten her hair wet. To make matters worse, she had just come from the beauty parlor where she had just gotten a perm for the big weekend.

"From what I could tell, the couple's car had a bad seal around their window or maybe it was down just a bit," recalled

Montgomery. "She, of course, saw it otherwise. I apologized and asked how I could resolve this."

"She said, 'I want you to fix my hair!'"

Montgomery worriedly asked her if she meant that he, specifically had to do her hair. No, she said, she preferred to return to the beauty parlor.

The woman and her husband left to have lunch at a fast-food restaurant next door. Montgomery found them there, apologized for what had happened, and refunded their money. Not only that, "I told her to have her hair done again and that would be on Mike's, too," said Montgomery. "They greatly appreciated this and continued to be regular customers at Mike's."

Terri Breining, the founder and CEO of Concepts Worldwide, a meeting planner, subscribed to the Nordstrom approach of encouraging empowered employees to use their good judgment.

"We don't attach a dollar value to good judgment," she said. "We tell our associates: 'You are a professional. We count on your good judgment.' We don't present them with a set of rules and some options. We believe that *everything* is optional—how they behave, the decisions they make, the recommendations they make. We constantly reinforce good judgment."

But, invariably, empowered people are going to use poor judgment. What happens then?

"I tell our people from the time they come to work at Concepts, that no one will ever be fired for making a mistake," said Breining. "If they make the same mistake several times, then we'll have another discussion. If you make a mistake and learn from it, then we're not going to have a problem. When they use poor judgment, we tell them so, and ask them how they would do something differently the next time. We walk through the situation with them and help them think through the process, so it becomes a learning opportunity. If the associate is unsure as to what to do next, Breining makes sure that a representative of senior management is available for a reality check. A senior manager will make a suggestion about taking care of the client, and will ask the employee what he thinks should be done. Then, we'll kick it around, and decide on the best direction to take. We never say, 'that's a stupid idea.' We always give them another option. Then I back that up with action. We don't throw tantrums or yell. People are treated like responsible adults and, surprisingly enough, they respond by acting like responsible adults."

In December 1999, when downtown Seattle was in chaos because of the rioting of protesters who tried to disrupt the meeting of the World Trade Association, there was at least one offbeat love story amidst the pandemonium. James Swift and Lucky Taylor had met in Paris at a chocolate factory, fell in love, and quickly decided to move to Seattle and get married. While staying at the W Hotel, Ms. Taylor stopped by the desk of cast member Dan Petzoldt to tell him that she was getting married.

"I asked her where she was going to have the ceremony and she said, 'That's one of the things I want to talk with you about,'" recalled Petzoldt. "She said that she wanted to be near the water. I asked her when she was getting married and she said 'tomorrow.' She and Mr. Swift had decided to elope and get it done during this exciting time in Seattle." Petzoldt was able to arrange for the ceremony and reception at Salty's restaurant in West Seattle, which has a spectacular view of downtown Seattle.

"As an afterthought, I asked her if there was anything else she would need," said Petzoldt. "She said, 'Yes. I need a photographer, flowers, and an appointment to get my hair done.'" As she listed all her needs, Petzoldt felt his eyes "getting bigger and bigger. But she was very calm about the whole thing. She knew it was unique and she was enjoying it, too."

Petzoldt asked Ms. Taylor if she had secured a minister, and indeed she had. But the minister called her a couple of hours earlier and told her that he was going to be participating in an anti-WTO demonstration and didn't know if he'd be done protesting in time to make the ceremony.

"We laughed about that," said Petzoldt. "As I turned to my computer to start searching for churches, Ms. Taylor told me that she had heard of a web site where you can go online and become an ordained minister over a period of time. I laughed. I thought it was a joke. But when she asked if I'd be willing to do that, I said I would."

At this point, Petzoldt had arranged everything else, so the minister was the last hurdle. He logged on to the web site, filled out the application, and the following day, he received his authorization. To add an additional challenge for Petzoldt, because the couple had met in Paris, when they wrote their own vows, a portion was in French. So Petzoldt had to be tutored in French pronunciation. Nevertheless, right on schedule, he married the couple, far away from the protesters and tear gas. He did all this with the backing of hotel manager Tom Limberg, who cheered on his empowered employee.

In every room at every W hotel, there is a telephone key marked "Whatever Whenever." When a guest presses that key, an empowered employee is ready to fulfill virtually any (legal) request. Cast members [the term for W employees] are told that if they are unable to get a guest whatever they want whenever they want it, then they've failed. W doesn't want those frontline people to go to a manager; they want those people to get whatever they need to make the guest happy. The manager is not going to be able to help them satisfy the guest; they should be able to do it themselves.

When a guest presses the "Whatever Whenever" key in the room, there's no telling what the request might be. One time, a reporter asked an employee at the W New York to locate a burial plot for his dog, which he claimed had just died. W found a pet cemetery on Long Island. On another occasion, a guest asked for enough chocolate to melt and fill a bathtub. W charged the guest for the cost of the chocolate but not for the expense associated with securing the chocolate, melting it, and getting it into the tub.

In early 1995, Continental Airlines made a conscious decision to empower its employees.

"We have guidelines that cover the way we want to handle whatever situations we can envision. But we tell our people that when something comes up that's not covered, we want you to make the decision that is not only good for the customer, but also good for the company. We're not interested in giving the customer everything he wants. If you'll do that, we'll be happy. Whatever you come up with," said retired chairman and CEO Gordon Bethune.

When Bethune was hired in late 1994 to turn around the carrier, the only way he could bring in the best people to help a failing company was to empower them. "I had to give 100 percent autonomy to the guy in charge of pricing," he said. "He didn't have to clear pricing with me. This really motivated him because he had never worked in an environment where he could call the shots. He would come to work here believing we were going to get the place fixed, but he also wanted to come to work in an environment where he had autonomy. That's a huge attraction. When you can get to say how things go on around here, that's how you buy into the team. We had to change a lot of middle management to get them to do it that way from then on."

Do these empowered people make mistakes? Sure. "If you make a huge mistake, we will show you the way we'd have preferred you handled it. You're not going to get in trouble for it," said Bethune, but "if you consistently can't make a good decision, we'll probably have to take you out of the decision-making process. But if a pilot landed long and went off the end of the runway into the mud, we're not going to make him a plumber."

Keys to Success

Regardless of the kind of business you are in, empowerment is always possible. In fact, it's not only possible, it's necessary. Good employees want to be empowered. They don't want to push papers or give rote answers; they want to have an impact on the future of their organization. Here's how great customer-service companies empower their people:

- Hire people who are looking to assume responsibility and ownership.
- Trust the people you hire.
- Give them the freedom to make decisions on the spot.
- Push the decision-making responsibility and authority down to the lowest level possible.
- Encourage them every step of the way.
- When empowered people use poor judgment, use those mistakes as tools for learning.

EXERCISE

What Does Empowerment Mean?

- Define the word "empowerment" and write down that definition.

- Compare that definition with the other people in the group.

- Ask yourself if "empowerment," as defined, exists in your organization.

- If so, write down all the ways that "empowerment" is illustrated in your organization.

- Once you have compiled that list, go over each of those illustrations of empowerment and discuss how they have benefited your organization.

- How can the value of empowerment become a core value of your company?

- How can you encourage employees to feel they are empowered?

EXERCISE

Empowering Compensation

- List all the ways that compensation and bonuses have an impact on empowerment in your organization.

- Discuss creative ways to use compensation to improve empowerment and entrepreneurship among employees.

7

Dump the Rules

Tear Down the Barriers to Exceptional Customer Service

The minute you come up with a rule you give an employee a reason to say no to a customer. That's the reason we hate rules.

—James F. Nordstrom, former co-chairman

As we discussed at the beginning of this book, when it comes to taking care of the customer, Nordstrom has only one rule for its employees: "Use good judgment in all situations."

Such simple direction makes life easier for individuals who respond to a straightforward customer service philosophy.

For some people, this corporate philosophy is thrilling! It's liberating! "Wow; my manager thinks I can make judgments of *any* kind—good, bad, or indifferent; and not only that, she's going to let me exercise my judgment." For others, being given just a single rule is terrifying.

In the early 1990s, when Nordstrom was hiring for its new store in the Washington, DC, suburb of Pentagon City, Virginia, the company received many job applications from individuals who had worked in the military and federal bureaucracies. One former bureaucrat actually told a Nordstrom executive, "If you give me a *hundred* rules, I'll be the best darn employee you ever had. But *one* rule? I don't think so." That kind of person doesn't want freedom; he wants to be told what to do. He feels more comfortable leaving his brain at home. Unless you are looking for an automaton don't hire that person.

"Because we don't have many rules, we don't have to worry about breaking them," a Nordstrom employee said. "We're judged on our performance, not our obedience to orders."

James F. Nordstrom, the beloved co-chairman, who passed away in 1996, hated rules because they got in the way of customer service and the Nordstrom philosophy of empowering employees. Jim felt that the more rules an organization has, the farther and farther it moves away from its customers. When that happens, the rules become the most important consideration to employees; not the customer. It's as if these unempowered employees wrap the rules around them like a security blanket, and then proclaim to the customer: "You can't hurt me. I'm protected by the rules."

Jim Nordstrom once said, "The minute you come up with a rule you give an employee a reason to say no to a customer. That's the reason we hate rules. We don't want to give an employee a reason—from us [management]—to say no to a customer. We feel that the majority of the people we hire want to do a good job and want to be successful. I think that's true of most companies." Jim felt that after people are hired, management at many companies do "vicious things" that turn off employees and take the fun out of people's jobs. "If you give them a hundred rules, you've taken away any empowerment that they can have."

Back in the days when Jim and his brother John N., cousin Bruce, and cousin-in-law Jack McMillan ran the company (from the late 1960s through the mid-1990s), Jim was fiercely protective of Nordstrom's freewheeling entrepreneurial culture and was willing to fight to do whatever it took to maintain it—even if it meant challenging employee grievances over wrongful termination. He once said, "I would rather we lost lawsuits from time to time than keep employees that are not up to our standards. Because a weak employee will make the others around him weak, and drag them down." With that in mind, the company tore up its rule book and told its managers, in Jim's words: "You can't rely on these rules. You can't sit back and wait for an employee to break a rule and then get rid of them. You have to sit down with them, one on one, and communicate."

Knowing they will receive full credit when things go well, and full blame when they don't, real Nordies enjoy their entrepreneurial, empowered freedom.

"I would never be comfortable in an environment where there are a lot of rules," said Van Mensah, of the men's clothing department in the Pentagon City store.

"Because we don't have too many rules," said salesperson Annette Carmony, "we don't have to worry if we're breaking them." Salespeople are judged on their performance, not their obedience to orders. Carmony recalled the time when a customer in her department misplaced a shopping bag containing three bars of soap that had been purchased in the lingerie department. "I went over to lingerie and got three more bars of soap and gave them to her. She thanked me and said, 'I can't believe you did this.'" The bars of soap were only 90 cents apiece, but they produced a happy customer.

That's Just the Way It's Always Been Done

During the course of our day, when *we* are the customers, we are constantly hit in the face with the rules, the process, the bureaucracy, the way it's always been done.

Why is that?

The simple answer is that most companies, organizations, governments, and so on are set up to make life easier for the organization—not for the customer. That's why those organizations have lots and lots of rules.

But we, as customers, don't care what your rules are. And while we're at it, we don't much care about the process, the bureaucracy, or the system either. We only want someone to take care of us.

Does your organization have a lengthy rulebook or employee manual or list of processes?

If so, does it help advance your organization to promote more attentive customer service? Probably not. There are actions you can take to change that situation.

For example, there is the action that Gordon Bethune took when he became chairman and CEO of Continental Airlines in 1994. Back then, Bethune was faced with a dispirited, mistrusting organization that had gone through a series of failed management regimes. Bethune knew that employee manuals were just a storehouse of regulations that were often created for legitimate reasons, but somehow eventually "spread far beyond their applicability and become calcified into dumb rote," he wrote in his book *From Worst to First*.

The Continental employee manual was a compilation of maddeningly specific rules and regulations that ranged from the shade of pencil that had to be used to mark boarding passes to the type of meals that could be served to delayed passengers. To make matters worse, the manual so specifically described job responsibilities that employees were unable to deviate from them for fear of punishment. The gate agent was forbidden from clearing up problems. The previous management had preferred that agents just stand there and feel the wrath of frustrated passengers. "Well, nobody likes to work like that. Nobody likes to be treated like a robot, like a little kid who can't solve a problem and make a contribution," wrote Bethune.

To dramatically make the point that things were going to be different from now on, Bethune needed to come up with a sensational symbol of changing times. One day, he assembled a number of employees, gave them copies of the manual and led them on a parade out to the parking lot. There, the employees summarily set the manuals on fire, a task they thoroughly enjoyed.

"And we sent word into the field that henceforth we wanted our employees to use their judgment, not follow some rigid manual," wrote Bethune. From that moment on, Continental employees were told that when they had to deal with a situation that was not addressed in their training, they were to follow one simple rule: "Do what was right for the customer and right for the company." Is that a conflicting message? No, just a complicated one. Bethune wanted employees who would neither blindly do everything for the customer without worry about expense, nor merely follow procedures that would alienate the customers. He wanted employees to consider both the interests of the customer and the interests of the company. The best way to deal with uncomfortable situations was to *use good judgment*.

Those of you who fly a lot are well aware of the longstanding controversy over the number and size of carry-on bags. Bethune says that when employees hide behind these rules they "don't have to take any indictment for their lack of customer service. I tell our flight attendant, 'if you can find room for that guy's bag, let's find it.' The flight attendant can do whatever he or she wants as long as it meets the federal air regulations."

After the manuals were literally and symbolically burned, Continental formed a task force of employees to evaluate every rule and regulation. The rulebook was replaced with more general guidelines for direction, rather than a rule for every inevitability, because Bethune knew that the rules would destroy the creativity of employees. "We started teaching the deployment of the *guidelines;* that's when it had the real meaningful effect," said Bethune, who said that the whole process was a learning experience for management. "If you make employees do the right thing, then they will. Our whole customer service emphasis has been first on treating our employees like they deserve everything we can do for them to do their job well, which includes letting them have some autonomy on how it's done."

Looking back on that bonfire in the parking lot, Bethune said he was of the opinion that, "Every company probably ought to burn their employee manual every now and then."

One summer not long ago, Robert Spector and his wife flew to Los Angeles, where Robert conducted some business. After renting a car at the Los Angeles airport, the Spectors spent a couple of days in Los Angeles, and then drove south to Orange County for a little rest and relaxation at the beautiful Ritz-Carlton in Laguna Niguel. One night, while they were driving around Laguna Beach, the icon for the engine lighted up on the dashboard. They consulted the owner's manual, which said that if the engine icon lights up, the dealer should be immediately contacted.

The following morning, Robert called the rental car agency and told them of the problem. The young man who answered the phone said, "Fine, drive the car back up to John Wayne Airport [a 45-minute drive up the freeway] and we'll give you a new car."

What? "First of all," Robert told the young man, "I'm on vacation. Second of all, we know there is something wrong with the engine of this car, and you want me to drive 45 minutes up the freeway. No, I want you to bring me a new car to my hotel."

His answer: "We can't do that. There's a rule against that."

Undaunted, Robert asked to speak to his supervisor. She eventually got on the phone and she didn't want to bring him a new car either.

"Look," Robert told the supervisor, "I write books on customer service. I speak to business groups all over the country about good customer service and bad customer service. And if you don't bring me a new car, in my next speech, I'm going to cite your company as an example of terrible service."

(Please feel free to use this line because it gets results.)

Forty-five minutes later, a new car arrived at the hotel. A friendly representative of the rental car agency handed Robert the keys to the new car, took possession of the keys to the old car, and drove off into the sunset.

Obviously, bringing a replacement car to the hotel could easily have been done. But it was much easier for this company to give their employees lots of rules and no discretion.

What kind of rules do you place in front of your employees? If you're an employee, what kind of company rules do you absolutely despise? Take the time to go through all your rules as if you've never seen them before. Evaluate each rule on its own merits. Was a rule instituted several years for some forgotten reason that no longer applies today. If that's the case, GET RID OF IT!

Richard Kessler, owner of the Kessler's Diamond Center stores in Milwaukee, Wisconsin, tells his employees to "Make decisions based on the values that we all agree that you believe in. If you make a decision based on those values, you're doing the right thing." His company's simple mission statement: "We are dedicated and committed to totally satisfying the needs of our clients based on integrity. If you follow our mission statement, you can't make a wrong decision."

At Realty Executives of Nevada, in Las Vegas, "We try to not have too many rules, and try not to have negative rules," said co-owner and president Fafie Moore. "I'm always telling people who work for me: 'If you can find a better way to do something, please come tell me about it. If we can eliminate something that we are doing so that it gives us more time to do something else that is more valuable in helping the customer, please tell me about it. If you go home and tell your husband or wife, "If I owned that company, this is what I would do," I want you to tell me that. That's how I get my most valuable ideas.' "

Follow the Golden Rule

The Mike's Express Carwash chain has boiled its set of rules down to the Big One: The Golden Rule. "We don't try to wear our employees down with a lot of rules. Everybody knows how they like to be treated when and where they spend their money," said Bill Dahm, president of Mike's, who said that this philosophy began with his father, who started the company in 1947. "My dad said that whenever we make a decision, we ask ourselves: 'How it will affect the customer? If I was in the customer's shoes, how would I feel?' We learned a long time ago that we're selling a service, and if we can do it really fast, they'll come back more often."

An appreciation of the Golden Rule is an essential aspect of employee training. "One way to really drive home to associates the kind of behavior you're looking for is to ask them to relate to how they feel when they go to a music store to buy a CD or go to Nordstrom to buy some clothes," said Dahm. "In our training, we spend a lot of time discussing experiences that our employees have had in other businesses. We talk about experiences that made them feel good, where they felt appreciated and felt they got their money's worth. We also talk with them about the kinds of places they've shopped where the salespeople treated them as if they were in the way. For example, one of our pet peeves is going to a store—where you want to spend your money—and the salesperson is talking to someone on the phone.

You're a paying customer, right there on the property, yet the person on the phone is getting all the attention."

Mike's, like Nordstrom, has a handbook that serves as a guide to things like benefits, as well as policies prohibiting stealing, smoking on the property, and so on, but when it comes to customer service, Mike's, again like Nordstrom, likes to keep it simple.

"The biggest thing we tell them to do is to exceed customers' expectations without slowing the operation down," said Dahm. "When someone gets his car egged, that stuff does not come off with a car wash. You have to use some compound and some wax to remove it. It wouldn't be uncommon for one of my associates to say to the customer, 'We're not too busy. Pull your car over here and let me clean it off for you.'"

Terri Breining, founder and president of Concepts World-wide, a meeting planning company, said that the contracts that Concepts Worldwide enters into with clients spell out the guidelines of exactly what the firm will do for the customer on a particular project.

But beyond the basic guideline, project managers are unencumbered with a lot of rules and are allowed "to do the job whatever way they want to," said Breining. "Each of our meeting planners has a different style of doing those things." Because of the individual styles of the project managers, clients can choose the manager they want to work with. "We've had experiences where a client and one of our meeting planners didn't get along. We don't have a rule that the client has to work with that particular planner."

Obviously, Concepts Worldwide, like every other business, needs to be profitable, and "We expect our project managers to make sure that their projects are brought in within budget, and that the clients are happy," said Breining. "But within those parameters, they are relatively free to do whatever they have to do—as long as it's not illegal or immoral."

Tom Limberg, general manager of the W Hotel in Seattle, said that "Good service is not about an employee with his head down looking in the three-ring binder rule of rules. We don't live in a world of black and white; we live in a world of gray, where we bend rules to fit customers. We don't bend customers to fit rules. That's what empowerment is."

FirstMerit: Decide on What's Best for the Customer

When John Cochran first arrived at FirstMerit Bancorp in 1995, he found an organization that was "very operationally oriented," he recalled. "It wasn't a marketing organization, which is what we are today. FirstMerit had all sorts of clearly stated procedures that were quite severe and radically customer unfriendly, and there were severe penalties for not following those procedures."

Ever since he assumed the position of chairman and chief executive of FirstMerit, Cochran has tried to eliminate as many rules as possible and to create a company that is "like Nordstrom, where employees are encouraged to use their common sense," he said.

Over the years, St. Charles Medical Center in Bend, Oregon, has made wholesale changes in its process simply by examining every policy and procedure—including the historic reason why a policy or procedure was implemented in the first place.

"For example," said chairman emeritus Jim Lussier, "quite often, we found that seven years ago something happened in the emergency room that had never happened before, and the emergency room supervisor at that time said, 'We need a policy about that.' So, somebody wrote a policy specifically about that particular incident. Years later, although that type of situation never occurred again, the policy was still on the books."

Therefore, St. Charles set about changing the mind-set and philosophy of procedures by empowering its caregivers. "We changed things by telling people: 'You're in charge of the situation. If you guys can stay within these fencelines and use the values of St. Charles, then you make the decisions you need to make. We'll support you every time. You don't need to look into a policy and procedure book about how to do that. Use your best judgment,'" said Lussier.

By trusting people to use their best judgment and telling them not be dictated by strict policies and procedures, St. Charles has found that "People are willing to crawl out on limbs and make decisions and muddle through a situation that is sometimes life-threatening," said Lussier.

In the process, the folks at St. Charles discovered an amazing thing. "We found that the quality people—the good, assertive folk that we have always relied on—weren't using all those policies and procedures anyhow," said Lussier with a smile. "In their own minds, they had already dumped the rules and were naturally using their best judgment. We were fooling ourselves that we had that kind of control."

Keys to Success

■ Trust the judgment of your frontline workers. If you don't trust them, why did you hire them?

Re-examine every rule and regulation in your organization. Let each rule stand or fall on its own merits. Do those rules and

(Continued)

(Continued)

regulations make sense in today's business environment? If not, dump them!

- Simplify the procedure that your employees take in taking care of the customer.

- Do what's right for the customer—and right for the company.

- When in doubt, do what Continental Airlines did: Burn your rulebook!

- Promote one main rule: The Golden Rule.

EXERCISE

Examine Your Rules

- Bring out your rulebooks, employee manuals, procedures, and so on.

- Assign a group of people to review all these materials.

- Ask them to write down all the rules, procedures, and so on that are internal—that is, not mandated by outside legislation, regulation.

- Compile that list and distribute it to all the people in your organization.

- Have people in your organization vote on those lists: What rules belong? What rules need to be eliminated?

- Eliminate all the rules that come between you and your customer.

8

This Is How We Do It

Manage, Mentor, and
Maintain Great Employees

I hear and I forget. I see and I remember. I do and I understand.

—Chinese Proverb

As we explained in Chapter 5, Nordstrom wants to hire men and women who are already nice and already motivated *before* they come to work for the company.

Nordstrom provides very little in the way of a formalized training program. And when asked who really trains his salespeople, chairman Bruce Nordstrom replied, "Their parents."

Once Nordstrom salespeople have gone through employee orientation and have become familiar with the culture, the systems, the merchandise, and the sales goals expectations, they are encouraged and empowered to find their own way of doing business. This book is entitled *The Nordstrom Way,* but there are actually some 50,000 Nordstrom ways, because each employee is an individual, with an individual style and approach to taking care of the customer.

Like competitive athletes, Nordstrom salespeople are motivated in a variety of ways to give extraordinary service because extraordinary service produces extraordinary sales volumes. The company regularly distributes videotaped interviews with top salespeople who offer tips and advice. Frequent staff meetings are used as workshops for salespeople to compare, examine, and discuss sales techniques, and to perform skits in which they play the roles of salesperson and customer. Top salespeople frequently talk to their colleagues about goal setting, marketing, selling, using the phone, and, of course, customer service.

The Importance of Mentors

It is up to managers and buyers to bring out the best in each of those employees. How is that done? Like everything else at Nordstrom, it starts with the initiative of each individual. Nordstrom has found that to achieve the top levels of sales performance, salespeople must have the requisite patience to gradually, over time, develop a personal clientele. They can build up their business by using the sales tools made available by Nordstrom—most important—by learning from other successful salespeople.

In other words, they are asked to find a mentor. They are encouraged to find a successful Nordstrom salesperson and watch how he or she does business. You can borrow the styles of several people and then take those ingredients create your own style. Again, that requires time and patience.

While new salespeople are encouraged to find mentors who have created and perfected their own sales tips and techniques, those new people are also encouraged to find their own niche, their own way of taking care of business because, ultimately, success at Nordstrom comes down to what works for each individual.

"Mentors are everywhere," say many top Nordstrom salespeople. Management encourages its top sales performers to mentor new salespeople.

As he was winding down his career at Nordstrom, "being number one was not as important to me as it used to be," said David Butler, a now-retired, top-performing shoe salesman from the Tacoma store. "It would have been very selfish of me not to share with other people what I was able to accomplish. I tried to help teach others what it takes to become a Pacesetter and give them the tools to do it. It was a lot more fun for me helping the entire department make their day, which helped the store make its day."

As we discussed previously, the Nordstrom culture is an essential part of what sets this company apart from all others. Those successful salespeople like David Butler, those mentors, embody that culture and transfer that culture to new Nordstrom associates. That's how this company has been able to thrive for more than a century, through four generations of management.

Find a Mentor

"You can observe a lot just by watching," Yogi Berra once said. That's why Nordstrom encourages new hires to keep their eyes open when searching for a mentor.

Leslie Martin, manager of the Fashion Valley store in San Diego, encourages new employees to "watch, observe, ask questions. That's part of empowerment. People will eventually develop their own style."

When Denise Barzcak started in sales at the Town Center mall store in Boca Raton, she found that the best training came from watching salespeople who were already successful. "We saw how they were so consistent. They were leading by example. You wanted to follow along, to be as good as they were because you were in the same situation. That core group motivated us throughout the training."

Leslie Umagat, a salesperson in the downtown Seattle flagship store, believed that the best employee training was informal, learning from the veteran salespeople on the department team and observing how they made their business happen.

Early in her career, "I worked with five Pacesetters at one time," she recalled. "It was difficult, and it was challenging. I was just starting. I had to find out what was my style and what would make my business happen. You can extract the things that work for you."

She learned quickly that a loyal customer always goes back to the same salesperson. In a department of five Pacesetters, each Pacesetter had her own loyal coterie of customers.

"I recognized which customers were loyal to which salespeople," said Leslie. "I built my base by keeping an open mind. When someone else's personal customer walked into the department, but that salesperson was not on the floor, I would say to myself, 'Yes, that's her personal customer, but how can I help that customer today?' I wanted to give the best service I could give on a consistent basis. I built my customer base on keeping my promises."

When Patrick McCarthy joined Nordstrom in 1971, he soon realized that he needed a mentor to teach him how to survive at Nordstrom. He eventually found his role model in a coworker named Ray Black, who was a professional men's wear salesman. Thoroughly knowledgeable about the merchandise, Black could take a swatch from a bolt of fabric that was going to be tailored for a suit and coordinate a complete wardrobe of shirts and ties, all the way down to the cufflinks.

Before joining Nordstrom, Black had worked for many years in several of downtown Seattle's fine specialty men's wear shops, and his loyal clients followed him from store to store. "They came into the department asking for Ray because he identified their needs and knew how to satisfy them," McCarthy recalled. "Men saw him as an ally. They heeded his advice on where to get a good haircut or what style of glasses to wear. He offered them choices and suggestions and gave them the confidence to try something different. Their wives saw Ray as the mediator who could interpret their views to their husbands."

McCarthy also noticed that Black had the ability to not only remember a customer's name, but his last purchase as well. (This was long before previous purchases became part of the store's computerized database.)

"I thought to myself, 'I want to be able to do that.'" So, Mc-Carthy volunteered to help Black whenever and wherever Black needed him, and the veteran salesman accepted the offer. "Pretty soon, we developed a routine: After Ray sold suits and sport coats to his customers, I helped them with their shirts and ties. With that increased customer contact. I was able to develop my poise and improve my interviewing skills."

Most important, Black taught McCarthy how to become an entrepreneur who could create his own business.

Black didn't sit around waiting for people to walk into the men's wear department; he was calling customers on the phone to alert them to new merchandise that was arriving in the store. "Ray showed me what a good salesman should be; he showed me that the Nordstrom system worked and that I could make as much money as I wanted," McCarthy recalled. "The way I saw it, the Nordstroms were taking all of the risks and providing all of the ingredients—the nice stores, the ambiance, the high-quality merchandise—to make it work. All I had to do was arrive every morning prepared to give an honest day's work and to value and honor the customer."

Over the rest of his career, as McCarthy rose to the top of the Nordstrom mountain, he became a mentor to many employees. (McCarthy's career and approach is examined in greater detail in Chapter 11.)

Van Mensah, who sells men's suits in the Pentagon City (Virginia) store in suburban Washington, DC, said that "Patrick McCarthy told me: 'Don't re-invent the wheel. Wait on one customer at a time. Be honest and sincere. Do what's right. There's nothing magical about this.' That's been my guiding principle. To make it work, you have to live it everyday. Make it your mind-set."

Mensah has gone on to become one of Nordstrom's top salespeople and he, in turn, has become a mentor.

"When we have a new store opening, I have been asked to fly in to meet with the salespeople in the men's wear area to talk about how to build a successful business," said Mensah.

That's how a culture is sustained, passing on the knowledge from one employee to another.

Setting an Example

That atmosphere of mentorship starts with the store manager, who understands the culture and is, in his or her store, the embodiment of the Nordstrom culture.

"You can't tell someone to go out and give good customer service, to go out and get a sales increase," said vice president Len Kuntz, who was once a store manager. "You have to tell them how to do it. Give the salespeople something they can use. For example, suggest that they send a thank-you note to a customer who brought back a return."

Leslie Martin, manager of the Fashion Valley store in San Diego, helps new managers find mentor-managers through a variety of ways, including brainstorming sessions. "I might do a managers meeting where somebody is really great in a particular area, such as planning special events or helping other people achieve their goals. That would give other managers ideas."

John Whitacre, the late chairman, used to tell managers that twice a day, for 60 seconds, they should look a fellow employee in the eye and tell that employee how much the manager cares about that employee, and the reasons why.

Encouragement

"Sometimes we push you, sometimes we pat you on the back," said Brent Harris, who was once a Nordstrom store manager and is now national merchandise manager for one of Nordstrom's shoe divisions. Harris believes in leading by example. "As a store manager, I wouldn't ask anyone to do something that I wouldn't do, whether stacking merchandise for a sale, or staying late." Harris would reiterate to the employees in the store: "Be accountable for what you do, work hard, and you can do whatever you want to do."

After they purchase the merchandise, buyers must "sell" it to their sales teams so that the sales teams can sell it to the customers. Buyers are always trying new ways to merchandise and share ideas with salespeople around the country during key times of the year, to share their thinking.

Communication with the sales staff is obviously an essential part of the buyer's job. Nordstrom's best buyers support the salespeople in the stores. The buyers work for the salespeople; the salespeople don't work for the buyers. That's what Nordstrom's Inverted Pyramid structure is all about.

Tammy Soltello, manager of the Savvy department in Mission Viejo, California, felt that, "as long as you make the customer happy, no one has a problem with you. If you make the customer unhappy, everybody has a problem with you. That's my mentality. I'm going to lead by example. Let's work together. We'll be a team. I'll show you how I multiple sell, how I suggestive sell. If you have two customers, turn the sitting room into a party. Let them show each other merchandise. Create a fun atmosphere. If you enjoy what you're doing they are going to love it. That's the mentality I use to build my team, a super-positive mentality. We are team oriented."

Customer service at Nordstrom is not just about selling clothes and shoes. "We're selling service, too," said Pat McCarthy. "We can convince customers that we are here to serve them—not just to take their money—by making their experience at Nordstrom easy. Sometimes, that means being the concierge. I get all kinds of requests that are not clothes-related. People ask me the name of a good hotel, or a nice place to have dinner, or where to get a massage. If I don't have the answer, I'll find out right away. Gas stations don't sell only gas; sometimes they sell directions."

A Kind Word

Although Len Kuntz has had a very successful career at Nordstrom, he has had his low points as well. Kuntz recalled when he was the beneficiary to some much-needed kind words. In 1989, Kuntz was given the assignment of managing the new $52 million, 280,000-square-foot Nordstrom store at the Fashion Centre at Pentagon City.

"The expectation level was high. We had just opened very successful stores at Tysons Corner Center [McLean, Virginia] and downtown San Francisco," Kuntz recalled. The Pentagon City store's opening was "the worst opening we ever had. No one came. It was the worst day of my life. I went home crying. I thought I was a failure."

But then John Whitacre, then regional manager of the Washington, DC area, sent Kuntz a note telling the young store manager how much he appreciated what he was doing and that "soon everyone will know what a great leader you are."

Nearly two decades later, Kuntz still has that letter.

Loyalty and Ownership

The Nordstrom family has always considered employee loyalty something to be earned, not expected. Because brothers Everett, Elmer, and Lloyd felt that the commitment to loyalty started with them, they wanted to provide an opportunity for their employees to make more money than any other retail salespeople.

"Some companies demand loyalty from personnel, but we felt that loyalty should come from us to them, first," said Elmer Nordstrom. "Loyalty is something earned, not expected."

Nordstrom's employee profit-sharing retirement plan inspires motivation and encourages loyalty. The company wanted to make it easy to retire for people who had done a great job. The program began in 1952 when the brothers wanted to make sure that employees would have money for retirement beyond Social Security, and to help the company attract better personnel.

"It was a natural development that reflected our basic philosophy: the better we treated our people, the better our people performed," recalled Elmer Nordstrom.

Today, with employment in most industries in such a state of flux, the only way people will be loyal to a company is if they are given appreciation, respect, good pay, and a piece of the action.

Nordstrom feels that even people who don't make it a career with the company can benefit from working there.

Pete Nordstrom recalled the time he was asked to discuss career choices with a young woman starting out in the business world.

"I told her that even if you don't know exactly what you want to do, Nordstrom is a good place to work because if you can come here and understand what it's like to interact with customers and do that well, then this experience is going to benefit you in some way. It's going to look good on your resume if you spent some time here and did well. Every company has a customer-orientation to it. We're fortunate to be known for that. So use that to your advantage. Learn something here. Do the best you can at it, and let it take you where it takes you."

How Companies Are Implementing Mentoring

Concepts Worldwide, the meeting planning company in Carlsbad, California, emphasizes the value of "mentoring unselfishly," said owner and founder Theresa Breining. "There has been a philosophy from the beginning that this is an organization where people can learn and grow personally and professionally. So, we take on people—and always have—who are motivated, have a great attitude, and want to do the job." Breining often tells new hires that she sincerely hopes that their future is with Concepts Worldwide. But in the event that they eventually move on, "if I am able to guide you in your chosen career, then I have done my job as a mentor."

Mike's Express Carwash takes the Nordstrom-like approach of promoting from within. Those veterans are Mike's best examples of customer service because frontline employees watch what the managers (as well as the owners) do to take care of the customer. "All of our managers are working managers," said President Bill Dahm. "We don't have offices for them. They are out there setting the example. That's what motivates our people: seeing that the person running their branch location is doing the same kind of customer relations that we expect out of them."

Mike's has consistently been voted Indianapolis's #1 Car Wash as voted by the readers of *Indianapolis Monthly* magazine.

When Gordon Bethune took over Continental Airlines in 1994, he found a dispirited organization that had been battered by a previous ownership that had played employees off against each other to win. That doesn't work well with teams. "We had been treating each other pretty shabbily," said the carrier's now-retired chairman and CEO. "How could you be at war with your employees and win?"

The Bethune regime began to turn things around first by treating employees with dignity and respect. In 1996, Continental hired the comedian Rodney Dangerfield—who was famous for the line "I don't get no respect"—to participate in an in-house training video. Bethune wanted employees to learn to treat each other with dignity and respect because that was a major step toward treating the customer with dignity and respect.

"We had the same employees here when we were the worst-performing airline as we did when we were selected as the best," said Bethune.

The difference was that Continental, like Nordstrom, found ways to manage, mentor, and maintain great employees by keeping them motivated, providing them with ideas, and creating an atmosphere where they could win and where they could provide great customer service.

Keys to Success

- Find ways to motivate your employees.
- Treat employees with dignity and respect.
- Utilize as training tools the people who have grown up in your culture.
- Encourage new people to find mentors.
- Promote a culture where people mentor unselfishly.
- Encourage managers to lead by positive example.
- Provide coaching tools.
- Promote a culture where people encourage each other.
- Promote a culture of loyalty and ownership.

EXERCISE

How Do We Develop Our Employees?

Gather a cross-section of your employees, both managers and front-line people. Talk about whether you have a culture that encourages and mentors new and long-standing employees.

Ask these questions:

(Continued)

(Continued)

- How do we manage our employees?
- How do we mentor those employees?
- How do we retain our great employees?
- How can we establish an internal mentor program (whether formal or informal)?
- How do we set a positive customer-service example for our employees and managers?
- Do we pat people on the back?
- Do we tell people they are appreciated?
- If the answer to those last two questions are "no," then how do we find a way to turn those answers into "yes"?

9

Recognition, Competition, and Praise

Create a Sustainable, Emotional Bond with Your Employees

There are two things people want more than sex and money . . .
recognition and praise.

—Mary Kay Ash, founder of Mary Kay Cosmetics

Nordstrom is an organization fueled by emotions. Motivated employees bring a passion to their business, a drive to succeed, a desire to sell, and a long-term devotion to serving the customer. Managers work to sustain this spirit by creating an emotional bond with their fellow employees through a potent blend of praise, recognition, and joy. And sometimes even tears.

At other companies, managers neglect to recognize the people they work with. They forget to give their people a pat on the back—and then those same managers are puzzled why their company has a reputation for giving bad service.

Nordstrom managers at every level work hard to make sure to let their colleagues know that they are appreciated.

"Recognition is so powerful, as long as it's as authentic and specific as possible," said Leslie Martin, manager of the Fashion Valley store in San Diego and a Nordstrom employee since 1982. Martin is also a past winner of the John W. Nordstrom Award, the company's highest honor, which is given to the employee who best exemplifies the characteristics of the founder. "Whatever their level of the Inverted Pyramid, employees want to feel needed and valued. Recognition reinforces the areas that we want to continue to focus on all the time, like service."

Recognition can be a very simple exercise.

"One of the greatest forms of recognition—because it means a lot to people—is just to walk up to them and thank them for a job well done," Martin noted. "When you tell them that a customer took the time to call or to write a letter about them, that means a lot. By recognizing those people, we reinforce the meaning of our Inverted Pyramid, by showing how important our frontline people are, because they are the ones who take care of the customer every single day."

When Brent Harris was a store manager, he made sure he knew the names and the faces of everybody who worked in his store. He says, "Being able to praise people is so important. It's the simple, personal things you say about them. You walk up to a salesperson and you say, 'I saw you had a 15 percent increase today. Good job!' That's powerful. You need to point out to others what makes that person a unique member of his or her department."

When individuals and departments have a successful day or are "on target" in reaching their sales goals, they are praised over the store intercom during the morning announcements before the store opens. The company rewards outstanding sales-per-hour and sales-per-month performances with cash prizes or trips, awards, and public praise for a job well done.

Executive Vice President and Regional Manager Len Kuntz recalled a lesson he learned from then co-president John Whitacre when Kuntz was managing the Northeast region.

"I had been there for three weeks. We were overbought; business was bad; morale was bad. John Whitacre called and asked me how it was going. I told him all the things I was doing and then he says, 'Are you writing a lot of notes to people? That's the first thing you should do. Find out some things that are going good.' I'm thinking, 'my house is on fire and he wants me to write notes.'"

Nevertheless, Kuntz started writing notes, finding opportunities to praise and recognize people, and gradually, the fortunes of the store turned around.

Recognition Meetings

One venue for reinforcing, recognizing, and rewarding behavior is the monthly Recognition Meeting, which is a feature of the Nordstrom culture. The surface objective of these meetings is to recognize outstanding sales performance, but they are also used to rally the troops and to get everyone excited about the performance of their teammates in their department, their store, and their region.

Kuntz decided to become a student of Recognition Meetings and sought ways of making them more engaging.

"When I was growing up in the company, I loved going to those meetings—even though they were terrible. Sometimes there was a goofy skit. Sometimes they were so dry; people just read [sales] numbers," said Kuntz. Nevertheless, the competitive executive enjoyed those meetings because they gave him ideas on how to become more successful. "I've missed only one Recognition Meeting at any level in my entire career, and that's because my daughter was born the night before. I almost went the next day, but my wife [Tonja Kuntz, also a Nordstrom executive] said she'd divorce me," he said, tongue in cheek.

When Kuntz became corporate sales-promotion director, he was given the opportunity to speak at Recognition Meetings around the country and saw how much they varied from region to region, depending on the personality of the manager who was running the meeting.

"The great thing about this company is the freedom you have to run your Recognition Meetings," said Kuntz. "No one tells you what to do. If you want to get up and sing, you can sing."

Attending a Recognition Meeting in the downtown Seattle flagship store on a June morning in 2004, an observer couldn't help but be caught up in the spirit of the event. Decorative yellow balloons were everywhere as several hundred top-performing managers and a few salespeople from the eight stores in Washington and Alaska, filed into the John W. Nordstrom Room, where the company holds its annual shareholders meeting and other large gatherings. It was standing room only. Throughout the room were signs emphasizing customer service:

- "We built this business one customer at a time."
- "Our customer service relationship is a fragile proposition. It's not elastic."
- "The question we should always be asking ourselves is this: Is the customer having an exceptional experience?"

The meeting is a pageant. Employees are honored for departmental sales increases, and for promotional ideas that drive sales increases. Customer Service all-stars are surprised by the presence of their parents or their spouse and children, whom Nordstrom brings to the meeting—unbeknownst to the honoree. The appearance of loved ones and the cheering of peers create an emotional bond among all in attendance.

"Recognition and praise are heartfelt and personal," said Chairman Bruce Nordstrom. "That recognition is better than a vacation in Hawaii. We put people in front of their peers and tell them that they are the kind of person we want others to emulate. We tell them we value and cherish their input to this company, and we wouldn't be as successful without that individual. That's strong stuff."

Also honored are departments that have sold the most of that month's featured item. Nordstrom loves to use intercompany competition as a tool for motivating the troops.

"We tend to manage by contest," said Executive Vice President Jammie Baugh. "When we have something we want to improve on, then we have a contest."

From their earliest days, the Nordstroms (all of whom are intensely interested in sports) initiated sales contests to promote rivalry among salespeople. If the store was overstocked in red pumps, for example, they would have a red pump selling contest, with the top sales performers rewarded with cash, flowers, dinners, or trips. "In a sense, every day was a contest," Elmer Nordstrom recalled. "Everyone tried to do their best, so that they wouldn't be stuck at the bottom of the list."

Each division in the company runs monthly MNS (Make Nordstrom Special) contests, where good ideas or suggestions—whether for sales or systems—are rewarded with cash. The winners are honored at the monthly Recognition Meeting.

According to Kuntz, a good Recognition Meeting encompasses four key aspects:

1. *Demonstrating sincere, authentic appreciation* for the people you are honoring. "That sounds obvious, but it's not very easy to do. Normally, most people in charge of meeting will give a generic description of [a salesperson who is being honored]. You need to talk about the essence of what a person does; what makes her different; how she adds value— that's important."

2. *Emphasize the team spirit.* "We want our people to say, 'I work for the greatest company in the world. I work for the greatest region in the greatest company in the world. I work for the best division/best department,'" and so on.

   "Part of our culture is that we compete. You can use that as a weapon. Where does our region rank within the company? When I got the Washington/Alaska region, we had room for improvement. We instilled the competition level and the pride, and we leveraged them to produce results."

3. *Teach people something new.* "I like to teach at least one specific subject or theme," such as sales techniques or promotional

ideas. "People really enjoy that. When I worked in our stores on the East Coast, many of our people had to take buses very early in the morning to be able to attend the meetings that started at 7:30. So, it was important to offer them something that would generate and maintain their interest."

4. *Perpetuate the culture.* "We discuss key points about our culture without it getting too convoluted or too long. We reinforce what makes Nordstrom unique and how the culture works for them."

Goal Setting

For all the people involved in sales, recognition comes from achieving goals. Goal setting binds every level of the Nordstrom organization. Salespeople, buyers, and managers are perpetually striving to meet personal, departmental, store and regional goals for the day, month, and year, and to surpass what they did during the same period a year ago. If a department fails to achieve one day's goal, the manager raises the following day's goal. Peer pressure and personal commitment push the most competitive employees toward constantly higher goals. Work shifts often start with a reminder of the day's goals; managers often quiz salespeople on their individual goals. A store manager (who earns bonuses based on sales increases and expense goals as a percent of sales) might rally the troops by getting on the public address system, before the store opens, to tell a story about someone who just sold $1,000 in cosmetics to one customer.

The company encourages a creative tension among its salespeople, who have ready access to sales figures from all departments and stores in the Nordstrom chain, so they can compare their performance with that of their colleagues across the selling floor or across the country. Each salesperson's semimonthly sales-per-hour figures are posted clearly for all employees to see.

The *Harvard Business Review* detailed one spirited 1979 sales-goal meeting, where the regional manager had asked every department manager and buyer to write down their sales targets for the following year:

> As the figures were called out, the regional manager wrote the amounts against the individual's name on a large chart. Next to the figure in turn was a space on which the regional manager had written his target for each manager. That target figure was kept covered during the initial part of the meeting in which the managers gave their target figures for the year.
>
> Then, amidst great excitement and suspense, the regional manager tore off the slip of paper, which covered his target for each individual manager. If the sales target of the manager was under that of the regional manager, the assembly would boo the unfortunate manager. However, if the manager's target was above that of the regional manager, then the group of persons would break out into cheers.
>
> One manager described the scene as being similar to a classroom during an exam, with all the store managers and buyers doing feverish calculations as they heard what their peers were setting as targets and were tempted to revise their own targets.

That scenario is not unusual; in fact, it's the norm. Every top Nordstrom salesperson is goal-oriented. Literally all of these stellar performers feed off of the recognition they receive from their customers and from Nordstrom, and they are motivated by reaching their goals. The best of the best set ambitious goals for themselves and when they meet those goals, they continue to set the bar higher and higher—and work harder and harder to sell more and more year after year.

At Nordstrom, the best salespeople achieve the status of Pacesetter. Pacesetters, who typify the entrepreneurial Nordstrom sales culture, meet or surpass the sales volume goal for their specific department for the one-year period from December 16 through December 15 of the following year. To maintain Pacesetter status, each year Nordstrom raises the target goal figures, depending on how many people achieved Pacesetter the year before. Generally, 8 to 12 percent of the salespeople in each division make Pacesetter.

Kazumi Ohara, who manages the Chanel handbags department in the downtown Seattle store, has been a Pacesetter for many years. To track her goal of reaching the Pacesetter target, Ohara divides the pay year by quarters, subdivides the quarters by six two-week pay periods, and then records her earnings for each pay period. She boosts her target level every year.

Pacesetters are given a personalized certificate of merit, business cards and note cards emblazoned with the Pacesetter designation, and a 33 percent store discount credit card (13 percent more than the regular employee discount) for one year, and cash, which varies, depending upon how many years the individual achieved Pacesetter status. After 10 years with the company, Pacesetters receive a Nordstrom stock award, which varies depending upon how many years they have achieved Pacesetter status.

Stephenie Melton, who sells women's apparel at the Fashion Valley store in San Diego, became a Pacesetter in her first year at the company in 1984. That year, she attended her first Nordstrom annual dinner honoring all Pacesetters. That night, "Somebody was being rewarded as a 20-year Pacesetter. Becoming a 20-year Pacesetter became my goal." Melton achieved that goal in 2004.

The company rewards other top performers with incentives such as cash and gifts. Every month, each store manager selects Customer Service All-Stars based on outstanding, consistent customer service, individuals' sales volumes and the level of support they give their coworkers. All-Stars are given a 33 percent store discount for one year. Based on three criteria—sales volume, customer service, and teamwork—Nordstrom rewards people with the best work shift schedule. The definition of the "best" shift depends on the individual. Some prefer the busiest times; others opt for shifts that best fit into their personal lives.

To qualify for the added recognition of being named a Pacesetter All-Star, individuals must be the top salesperson in their goal group, measured on a company-wide basis. In addition, they must have been in the same goal group for the entire payroll year to be eligible for this special recognition.

Pacesetters who surpass one million dollars in sales volume for the Pacesetter year, earn membership in the exclusive Million Dollar Club. In 2003, 50 employees made the club, up from 32 the year before.

Commission Sales versus Customer Service

Some might feel that there is a dichotomy between giving spectacular customer service and earning commission sales. It's true that, in some cases, salespeople are happy to get the sale and are even happier to move on to another customer. They don't see themselves in a long-term relationship with a customer because they don't see themselves in a long-term relationship with their job.

At Nordstrom, top salespeople argue that because their compensation is linked to satisfying the customer, it's in their best interest to act responsibly. The best Nordstrom salespeople know that if they take care of the customer, the dollars will follow. But they can't look at the customers with dollar signs in their eyes. With Nordstrom's liberal, virtually unconditional, money-back return policy, if people aren't happy with what they've purchased, they are going to bring it right back. That means that everyone's time is wasted—the salesperson and the customer. "A happy customer will refer me to her friends," said a retired Nordstrom salesperson. "She won't do that for someone she feels doesn't have her best interests at heart."

And as Patrick McCarthy pointed out, "I want to make sure that the customer leaves with everything he needs. But I don't think about the cash register; it'll always be there."

The Customers Always Write

At Recognition Meetings, customers' letters of appreciation are read and positive achievements are recognized, while coworkers stand up and cheer for each other.

For example, here's one about salesperson Melinda Mason. A customer wrote:

> You should think strongly about promoting this woman. I am deaf, and I wanted slippers for my mother. I left the old slippers in my other car. Melinda called my husband for me (I can't use the phone), got the size, and talked him into shopping for dinner for us (no time in my schedule today to shop) and cooking it!

Nordstrom executives read all the letters that come in from customers, attach notes for the store managers to review. Kuntz said that he handwrites 60 notes to salespeople who are mentioned. "I usually get back letters from those people. One salesperson whom I didn't know wrote back to me and said her husband had framed the note from me and put it on their refrigerator."

Letters of complaint about Nordstrom's customer service are also read over the store intercom (omitting the names of the offending salespeople). "That's how we learn that the customer is our boss," said Patrick McCarthy. "Nordstrom's name is on my paycheck, but I'm paid by the customer."

Today, the signature on employees' paychecks reads: "Blake Nordstrom on behalf of the customer."

Implementation Lessons from Other Companies

At Mike's Express Carwash, "We constantly remind our people that the customers make this all possible," said President Bill Dahm. "We tell them, 'We sign your paychecks, but when the people that you've given good service to come back time and time again, they are making all this possible.' Repeat business is what makes this thing work."

Mike's constantly reinforces its commitment to customer service by reading customer comment cards—both good and bad— at employee meetings. And Mike's answers every one of those customer comment card because part of a company's commitment to customer service is reinforcing that commitment with its customers.

A review of the letters that Mike's receives from customers shows that the vast majority have to do with small but significant things: scuffs and dullness on the hood and roof; an emblem missing from the front grille of a car; dissatisfaction with the way an employee operated a customer's stick-shift. Those things may be small, but when it happens to you, they become significant. In each one of those instances, Mike's employees made sure the customer received satisfaction, and in virtually every instance, the customer was taken care of without a frontline employee having to ask his or her boss for permission because the employees know they are supported by their management's 100 percent commitment to customer service.

Gordon Bethune, retired CEO of Continental Airlines, believes that part of his job is recognizing great individual performances. "Every time a customer writes me and commends an employee, not only will I write back to the customer, I will also handwrite a little note to the employee, underline the nice things that were said, and write thank you. Because we get a lot of nice letters, I do a lot of that—and it pays off," he said. If flight attendants and other employees who have personal contact with customers, receive five such letters, Continental hands out a special star to be worn on their uniform. "People know that you are being recognized as someone who gets a lot of accolades."

"Recognition and praise are the best motivators I know. When you recognize and praise your people, they will go out and do anything for you," he said. "Every time you talk to me you're going to hear me talk about my team and how wonderful they are, and what they did."

Keys to Success

■ Always find an opportunity to praise employees for great acts of customer service.

■ Recognize and reward those great acts.

(Continued)

(Continued)

- Use financial rewards to encourage customer service.

- Provide your employees with information on how they are doing—and how the competition is doing.

- Sent notes of praise to employees who give great customer service.

EXERCISE

Praising Your Employees

- Ask each person to think of a fellow employee—a peer or someone who works for you or with you—who gives great customer service.

- Write a note of recognition and praise for that person.

- Send the note to that person.

EXERCISE

Organize Recognition Meetings

- Select a committee to create and organize the meetings.
- Organize an agenda.
- Decide on a purpose and objective for the meeting.
- Create awards and other forms of recognition.
- Have the meeting.

(Continued)

(Continued)

- Videotape the meeting so that the committee can critique it later.

- Distribute feedback forms to those in attendance. Get their comments on the meeting, and incorporate those suggestions into the planning for the next meeting.

EXERCISE

Make Your Company Special

- Create a contest similar to Nordstrom's Make Nordstrom Special, where employees are asked to come up with promotions and suggestions to drive results.

- Create a good reward for the winners.

- Make this contest a regular part of your culture.

EXERCISE

Goal Setting

- Assemble several of your people from all departments of your company.

- Direct those people to brainstorm on company goals, both individual and collective.

(Continued)

(Continued)

- Compile an official list of those goals and distribute them to everyone in the organization.

- Find ways to reward individuals and departments who achieve those goals.

EXERCISE

Customer Feedback: Letters

Do you get letters from customers?

- Collect those letters—both positive and negative.

- Edit them.

- Distribute those edited letters to your colleagues.

- Act upon the suggestions that customers have made in those letters.

- Use those letters to help create a customer service culture in your organization.

PART III

WHAT EMPLOYEES CAN DO TO CREATE NORDSTROM-STYLE SERVICE

This part examines the role of the people on the frontlines of your organization, and the influence they wield in making your company a customer-service organization.

First of all, frontline people must buy into the culture and understand their role in maintaining and supporting the culture through their actions.

Frontline people are generally the ones who come in closest contact with your customers. Therefore, they are crucial to your organization's ability to give customer service. They must be empowered to establish relationships with your customers and to find ways to take care of your customers in every way possible. They must be able to listen to the customer, understand the customer's needs, and follow through with whatever needs to be done.

Frontline people must have a thorough knowledge of the products and services your organization offers because it is

189

through those products and services that relationships are created, nurtured, and maintained.

Frontline people must be team players because it is through teamwork that cultures are formed and sustained.

In this part, we see the value and the importance of the individual within the organization, and how each person—who is honest, ethical, hardworking, and empathetic—can help to create a customer-service culture.

10

Sell the Relationship

How Frontline Salespeople
Create Lifetime Customers

*We are each of us angels with only one wing, and we can only fly
by embracing one another.*

—Luciano de Crescenzo

In your company do you value relationships? Do you have an organization that promotes a culture where building and maintaining relationships with customers are essential elements to your customer-service philosophy?

Patrick McCarthy is Nordstrom's all-time top salesperson. Until he retired in early 2000, after 29 years with the company, Pat was the quintessential Nordstrom employee. For the last 25 of those years, Pat sold men's tailored clothing in the downtown Seattle store, and was Number One in sales throughout the chain for an astonishing 15 years in a row. An entrepreneurial self-starter like all top Nordstrom salespeople, McCarthy, who considered himself "a franchise within a franchise," was undoubtedly the best-known salesman in Seattle. Drawing from a personal client list of 7,000—from recent college graduates to chief executive officers to United States senators—he racked up well over $1.5 million in sales every year.

Pat tells the story of playing golf one day with a couple of people who didn't know who he was. At the first tee, one stranger who was in his foursome asked the typical question: "What do you do for a living?"

To which Pat replied: "I sell a relationship."

The questioner looked at Pat kind of funny, and returned to the golf game. But at the second hole, he had to ask the question again: "No, really, what do you do for a living?"

Pat replied: "I sell men's suits at Nordstrom."

"Oh, so *that's* what you do," said the stranger, fully satisfied with the answer.

"No," Pat replied. "That's not what I do. What I do is sell relationships."

And that's exactly what most successful businesses and salespeople do: *Sell relationships.* It is axiomatic that people like to do business with people they like. If your product or service is similar to your competitor's, and the price for that product or service is similar to that of your competitor, what will be the reason why you will get the business and not your competitor? The answer to that question is the relationship you have with your customer and the trust you have built up over time. Once you've established and nurtured that relationship, why should your customer go anywhere else?

McCarthy's first indication of the value of selling a relationship came when he first joined Nordstrom in 1971 and saw how Ray Black, then the company's most successful men's clothing salesman, had made a successful living from the relationships he had developed with his customers. Black taught McCarthy the value of something as simple as remembering customers' names. Black had the ability to recall a customer's last purchase. He would make suggestions for purchases and offer choices.

Black was so good that customers would come into the Nordstrom men's wear department and ask for him. If he wasn't working that day, they would leave and come back on a day when he was working.

Create Relationships While You're "Measuring Both Feet"

For many years, a Nordstrom executive named Pat Kennedy oversaw the company's men's shoes division, which accounted for about a quarter billion dollars in sales. Year in and year out, Kennedy's division had some of the best financial performances of any other division in the Nordstrom chain.

Someone once asked the since-retired Kennedy what he instructed the salespeople in his division to do in order to produce such results. His answer was a line that he heard often over the years from one of his mentors, Bruce Nordstrom: "I tell them to measure both feet."

Measure both feet? In the literal sense, a knowledgeable shoe salesperson will measure both feet because she knows that a customer's right foot might be a slightly different size than the left foot. So, by measuring both feet, she is showing the customer that she knows what she's doing.

"People need to understand the dynamics of how you actually measure a foot," says Jack Minuk, vice president of women's shoes. "How do you put a shoe on a customer that actually fits the foot? Even though a customer may measure a certain size, in reality, there is no universal fitting standard in the footwear industry. With our hands-on training, our people understand the nature and anatomy of the foot to best fit her feet."

When a customer has over a size-and-a-half difference between shoe sizes for her right and left feet, it has been a Nordstrom policy for many decades to split sizes so that the customer doesn't have to buy two full pair of shoes.

Just as important as the actual measurement, is the salesperson's taking the time to talk to the customer and to begin planting the seeds of a relationship by asking pertinent questions: What kind of business are you in? Are you on your feet all day? Do you need dress shoes or more casual shoes? Do you play sports? Do you need shoes for those activities? Do you have foot problems? All the while, that salesperson is creating a relationship by taking note of what the customer is telling her.

What do you do in your business to create a relationship? When it comes to customers, new and old alike, how do you—metaphorically speaking—measure both feet?

Listen to the Customer

For successful salespeople like Leslie Umagat, the process of customer service "starts by just listening to the customer. Determine what her needs are and provide solutions through the resources and merchandise that you have."

Salespeople who develop an understanding of customer service the Nordstrom way have taken the time to grasp the intricacies of the system and to customize it to their own personality and talents. "The best salespeople in Nordstrom have found, through trial and error, what they do best," said David Butler, a retired shoe salesman who worked in the Tacoma store. "Not everybody can be a Pacesetter, but everybody has certain strengths." Top salespeople believe in making customers your best friends. Added Butler, "Treat customers like royalty and let them know that you will take care of them. Customers are here to spend money, so make them happy."

At Nordstrom, customer service means treating each customer as an individual, learning the customer's likes and dislikes, and treating her as a whole person. Customer service comes from the heart. Then individual salespeople add their own personal touch, creating a situation where the customer feels as if she is working with a friend, rather than just a salesperson.

The Personal Book

Personal books have been a part of the arsenal for Nordstrom salespeople for many years. In the old days, personal books were loose-leaf notebooks that contained vital information on every customer, including phone numbers, credit card numbers, names of spouse and children, previous purchases, sizes, vendor preferences, likes and dislikes, special orders, and any other characteristics, such as being a difficult fit or preferring to shop during sales events, and so on. Today, personal books are no longer physical notebooks; they are all computerized in a customer-service software package.

"The physical personal books were good, but sometimes very inconsistent. This allows more consistency and, therefore, better relationships," said Brian Townsend, store manager of the Tacoma Mall. "The more information we can remember about our customers, the easier it is for them to shop." By remembering pertinent information about their customers salespeople become more closely connected with those customers.

According to an internal Nordstrom survey, the company's million-dollar-sales salespeople said that 68 percent of their business comes from personal trade, which makes the personal book an invaluable tool.

If Stephenie Melton can't find an item that a customer has requested, she makes sure she gets back to that customer because "if you follow through, you will have a customer for life. They know that you put the time in to find what they were looking for. Don't drop the ball. A customer is looking to do business with someone they can trust."

Christerlyn Williams is a Nordstrom salesperson in the Michigan Avenue store in downtown Chicago. One day, a customer expressed interest in a leather coat in one of the women's wear departments. The customer, a bargain shopper, told Christerlyn, "I love the coat but it's way too expensive. But if it ever goes on sale, will you let me know." Christerlyn said she would do that and took the customer's business card.

"I just kept the list and when I would go through my personal book, I would see her name. I was waiting for that coat to go on sale, and when it did, I called her." Needless to say, the customer was happily surprised; overwhelmed. Christerlyn shipped the coat to her directly.

"That was the beginning of our relationship," said Christerlyn.

"Christerlyn, to me, is very special," said the customer. "The first thing I do when I come to her department is ask for her. She is very willing to do more than I expect and she connects with me very well."

As for Christerlyn, whenever the customer tells her that she's coming into the store, "I can't just stay in my own department. I have to move around and go from department to department because I know she needs panty hose, she needs a scarf, she needs something. And I'm going to be the one to sell it to her because she's my customer."

Nordstrom salespeople like Christerlyn and Stephenie and the others featured in this book take ownership of the customer. But what's even more remarkable about the Nordstrom culture is how customers feel about Nordstrom salespeople. When Robert Spector speaks to business groups, invariably someone in the audience will come up after his presentation and start the conversation by saying, "I have this Nordstrom salesman," and proceed to tell a story about outstanding customer service—either one spectacular example or just a description of good, solid, steady service over the course of several years.

In most sales cultures, salespeople are always claiming a customer as their own. But when a customer claims a salesperson as his or her own, that's powerful; that's a relationship.

Beyond Sales

Top salespeople don't look for the one spectacular sale that will make their day. Instead, they are committed to planting the seed for an ongoing business relationship and doing what's necessary to regularly nurture that seed.

Sometimes great customer service at Nordstrom has nothing to do with making a sale that day.

For example, there's the extra service that Kathleen Tardie, who sells in the Nordstrom store in the Tacoma, Washington Mall, did for one of her regular customers. In a letter to store manager Brian Townsend, the customer wrote: "This last week I called Kathleen with a problem that had absolutely nothing to do with Nordstrom." The customer had gotten her hair colored by her usual hair stylist "and walked away horrified at the job she had done." So the customer called Kathleen Tardie "because she always looks great, and she never would let me walk away from her looking awful, even if it cost her a sale." Kathleen called her own hair stylist and booked the customer in for an appointment the next day. "The true sign of a person who has their clients' best interest at heart is going the extra mile to help without any expected return," the letter concluded. "The only return I can offer is sharing with you my warm feelings for Kathleen and the services she provides, and continuing to be a loyal customer."

Product Knowledge

You can't develop the relationship if you don't know your product. That's why all the top Nordstrom salespeople place a high value on product knowledge. The company encourages them to keep up with product specifications, product changes, fashion trends, and other industry information through seminars, demonstrations, videos, and, occasionally, first-hand looks at how the products are constructed.

Salespeople are expected to promote product features, advantages, and benefits to match the customer's expressed needs and wants. One of the Nordstrom mandates to salespeople is to promote "fit first" because if the product doesn't fit, nothing else matters. In addition, salespeople are asked to provide immediate feedback to the department manager on merchandise, quality, fit, and product availability, so that the manager can respond accordingly.

Salespeople need to "get excited about the product," said David Butler. "Too often, salespeople start daydreaming when they are talking to the customer, then they wonder why they didn't sell that shoe. If you're not interested, why would you expect the customer to be interested? Why should I buy something from a salesperson who doesn't care?"

Denise Barzcak believes in the cliché "knowledge is power." She feels that a salesperson "should know everything about the item—the fabric, the cut, the fit—which gives you credibility."

Top Nordstrom salespeople do not confine their product knowledge to their own department. They take advantage of Nordstrom's policy that allows salespeople to sell anything in any department throughout the store, by learning about the products in those departments.

"I have a lot of men that I sell everything to, including shoes," she said. "Now, I help a lot of women who are the spouses of my clients. They like the way I take care of their husbands, so they ask me to take care of them."

Although product knowledge "enhances the customer-service process," Leslie Umagat believes that you can't be a successful salesperson until "a rapport or a connection has been built. Without that connection, I don't believe product knowledge can be imparted successfully. The underlying foundation is the connection between me and the customer. And then you can go on with the rest of the process."

Honesty and Sincerity

Besides product knowledge, Van Mensah of the Pentagon City store, believed that honesty and sincerity are the keys to success.

"When you are dealing with the kind of clients who come to Nordstrom, if you try to play games, they will see through that very quickly," he said. "If you know the merchandise is not right, come forward and say, 'in my professional opinion, this is not going to work for what you are buying it for.' You might lose some money; it might be the most expensive item he wants to buy. But I would rather sell something that is inexpensive, that will actually work better for him. If you tell him the product is not right for him, you get more credibility."

His reputation among the Washington, DC, power elite has earned Van a place in the Pentagon's Executive Transitional Assistance Program, which helps soon-to-be-retired senior officers—generals, colonels—learn how to transition into civilian life. Van conducts the "professional image" segment of the program for these officers, who are brought into Washington from military bases around the world. Mensah frequently gets follow-up calls from these officers who need a suit for a meeting or a job interview.

When it comes to selling suits to congressmen and senators, Mensah is strictly bipartisan. He was given presidential cufflinks by a former cabinet member, and was invited to George W. Bush's presidential inaugural in 2001 by a former senator who was on the transition committee.

Asked to describe his proudest moment working at Nordstrom, Van recalled the time he received a phone call from a customer who had rushed to get a flight to Washington for a wedding, only to discover that he had somehow packed the pants from one suit and the jacket from another suit. "Van," said the customer over his cell phone, "I'm in big trouble."

Because Van knew the customer's size, he made sure a new suit was ready—including alterations—when the customer arrived at the store, with his limousine waiting. Not only that, Van noticed the customer's belt looked old, so Van sold him a new belt. Fifteen minutes later, the customer was on his way to the wedding.

Building a Business from Scratch

How does one build a personal business from the ground up? That kind of challenge faces Nordstrom employees who open stores in regions of the country where Nordstrom had not previously been. Often these pioneering employees don't have the luxury of calling on friends or relatives to help them build up their business. They must find other ways to build up their clientele one person at a time. They develop a personal book of customer data (more about that later in this chapter), they send thank-you notes, they make a lot of phone calls, and they work hard at developing long-term relationships with customers.

When Theresa Lopez Malof began building up her business in the Fashion Valley store in San Diego, she took advantage of her contacts in the local Mexican-American community. Her ability to speak Spanish "comes in handy and can really be an advantage."

"It's very important for me to treat my customers the way I want to be treated, with professionalism," said Theresa. "If you do that, the customer will always come into the department looking for you to take care of them. I have customers who tell me: 'I like your look. I want to dress just like you. The next time you get something like [what you're wearing], put it aside for me.'"

Don't Judge a Customer by Her Shoes

Although it's important to pick up on what the customer is wearing, veteran Nordstrom salespeople caution that snap judgments that are based on a customer's appearance can cause you to lose out on a potentially lucrative sale. For example, when Patrick McCarthy was working at the Tacoma store in the 1970s, a woman in her fifties walked through the sportswear department one morning dressed in tacky clothes and a pair of old white tennis shoes with a hole in the toe. There was no stampede to wait on her. After a few minutes went by, McCarthy came over to say hello. Two hours later, she had purchased about $5,000 [in 1970s dollars] worth of sport coats, shirts, and, sweaters, which, she explained, were uniforms for the crew of her boat. She asked McCarthy to put all the items together for her driver to pick up. The customer turned out to be the daughter of a famous American industrialist, and was on her way to her estate in the San Juan Islands. "That was a tremendous learning experience," said McCarthy. "Never judge a book by its cover; open it up. If you treat a kid who is buying a $19.95 belt the same as a businessman buying a $1,995 Oxford suit, you will be successful. That kid might become a customer for life."

Sales Tools

The tools that Nordstrom provides its salespeople contribute to their individual success. One of the most important tools is the telephone.

When Joe Dover was a Nordstrom shoe salesman, he had a special way of following up with a customer who had just bought a pair of shoes from him. A couple of days after the purchase, Dover would call the customer and ask how the shoes were working out. "Ninety percent of the time, they're so stunned that you called that they remember you," said Dover. He would then invite the customer to Nordstrom to get his shoes shined (Dover picked up the tab). That offer got the customer back into the store, where Dover would have the opportunity to sell him another pair of shoes—or at least stop by and stay hello.

The telephone is an essential tool for Van Mensah. His 3,000 active customers include many international business people and government officials.

"Some clients call me from their office, or overseas, or from their plane," says Mensah. "They'll say, 'I'm coming in from Europe and I need a suit and tie. I'm going to be in Washington for only a few hours and I have to fly to another location. Could you put this together for me?'"

Not surprisingly, whenever he's not selling a customer in the store, Van is on the phone. He generally makes 25 to 30 customer calls per day. All the top performers at Nordstrom do the same thing.

Relationships with Vendors

At Nordstrom, the importance of relationships extends to its vendors.

"Our vendors play an active role in our business all the way to the selling floor," said Jack Minuk. "We rely heavily on their expertise. We want our vendors to have relationships with our salespeople and department managers. We want their involvement and guidance in terms of presentation. We want them involved in product knowledge clinics with our salespeople. We want them fully vested, so they feel that this wonderful customer-service machine we have at Nordstrom is very acquainted with their product."

Nevertheless, Minuk readily conceded, "That's not to say that we're easy. We can be challenging. We hold our vendors accountable. Product is everything. Loyalty is required; it's not optional."

Nordstrom is well known for taking a chance on a vendor, nurturing that relationship, and helping that vendor grow—not only within Nordstrom, but also within the retail industry. One example is Steve Madden, the shoe company. Founder Steve Madden told *Women's Wear Daily,* "Clearly there would not be a Steve Madden brand without Nordstrom. . . . They allowed entrepreneurs like myself to have a national base."

Ever since 1992, the company awards its Nordstrom Partners in Excellence Award to vendors "whose products and business practices best exemplify our commitments to quality and value, service and integrity." Nordstrom wanted to find a way "to recognize the people who do it the best; people who not only make the best products but are honest and ethical and really a pleasure to be partners with; people who care about our success and people whose success we care about," said Bruce Nordstrom.

Past winners include the Estée Lauder Companies, Tommy Bahama, Josie Natori, the Hickey Freeman Company, and the Dexter Shoe Company.

Implementation Lessons from Other Companies

The real estate business in Las Vegas is one of the most competitive in the country. For Fafie and Jeff Moore and their team at Realty Executives of Nevada, most of the business comes as a result of referrals through relationships with coworkers, neighbors, and friends because "that's where the client's greatest comfort is," said Fafie.

"One good referral can generate four or five sales," said Jeff. "That represents the lifetime value of the client. For an agent who can gain the respect and trust of the customer, the lifetime value of that one customer could represent a significant annual income each year. One customer can account for hundreds of thousands of dollars of income—if it's handled correctly. You only need a handful of foundation customers that can spread to bigger customers."

In an effort to build relationships, Realty Executives asks its agents to track their "spheres of influence"—satisfied clients who would recommend their services—and to keep in regular contact with those people, because you never know when that relationship might lead to a sale. A referral that comes from a satisfied client is a lot easier to get than new business from a stranger.

One of Realty Executives' most successful independent agents is a bundle of energy named Laura Worthington, whose job far transcends selling someone a house. She is there to take care of them every step of the way—even after the paperwork for the house has closed.

"I tell people: 'I'm your real estate consultant for life. If you have questions, I am always accessible. I will help you," said Worthington, a busy wife and mother of three. "Somebody once said, 'Laura doesn't just sell houses to people, she bar mitzvahs with them.'"

Now, *that's* a relationship.

At Callison Architecture, "Many decisions are based on long-term rather than short-term benefit," said company president Robert Tindall. Founder Tony Callison, who founded the firm in 1973 and who passed away in 1988, created a philosophy embedded in these 10 relationship-building principles:

1. Give the clients more than they expect.
2. Leave them something to remember you by.

3. Think the project (problem) through.
4. Ask yourself: "If I were the client, would I pay for this?"
5. Don't give reasons why it can't be done. Tell how it *can* be done and the consequences.
6. Don't wait to do it if it can be done now.
7. Service the client not the project.
8. You don't know if you don't ask.
9. Start a conversation with one new person every day.
10. Sketch ideas being discussed in front of the client. Always bring tracing paper and scale.

"With companies that we've had long-term relationships with, we have to constantly reinvent ourselves so that we don't become lazy and give them what we've always given them. It's a constant challenge. It's easier to grab a new client and wow them. The work begins after a few years when they are thinking, oh, we've been with these guys," said M. J. Munsell, a principal in Callison. "There are a lot of people knocking on our clients' doors. We have to remind ourselves every day that we are in constant competition with those other firms."

To guard against this complacency, Callison has tried several approaches. "One way might mean introducing new people in the firm to the client or providing the client with new services or a new product that they are not expecting from us," said Munsell. "It might mean changing the way we present to the client. That's how we invigorate our staff. We tell them: 'Don't just give us the same old thing. What can you do new for this client today that you didn't do for them yesterday?' By tackling this problem, we can have creative fun and do new things in the process."

Another way to keep things fresh is to be a source for new ideas and approaches. Callison devotes a lot of time and energy into researching the industries of their clients and trying to figure out where those industries are going. Just as Nordstrom sales-people maintain relationships with their customers by sending them thank-you notes after a sale, Callison employees will clip out articles on subjects they think their client would be interested in.

Keys to Success

Relationships are the essence of customer service. If what you are selling is similar to what your competitor is selling, and if your prices are similar to your competitor's prices, how can you get an edge? By developing a strong relationship with your customer—and by never taking that relationship for granted. Customers are looking for people who take responsibility for their actions. Those customers can be very forgiving if they see that you hear the problem and you take care of the problem.

- Listen to the customer.
- Understand the customer's needs.
- Emphasize knowledge of your products and services.
- Be honest and sincere.
- Track your sphere of influence.
- A referral that comes from a satisfied client is a lot easier to get than new business from a stranger.
- Create a lifetime experience.
- Develop a positive working relationship with your vendors and suppliers.
- Service the client not the project.
- Become a source for new ideas.
- Take responsibility.

EXERCISE

Measuring Both Feet

How do you develop a relationship with your customers?

- Gather a cross section of your colleagues for a brainstorming session on how you develop the relationship.
- Prepare a list of questions that you ask your customers.
- Distribute this list to everyone in your organization.
- Ask them to add to this list.
- Make this list of questions a standard feature in your training.

EXERCISE

Tracking Spheres of Influence

How did you get that client?

- Make a list of your longest standing customers.
- Ask them what's keeping them with your company.
- Devise ways to reward those clients for their loyalty.
- Follow through by rewarding them for their loyalty.

EXERCISE

Rewarding Vendors and Suppliers

- Make a list of your best vendors and suppliers.

- Devise ways to reward them for their loyalty.

- Emulating Nordstrom's "Partners in Excellence," create an official program to reward your vendors and suppliers.

11

The Sale Is Never Over

Secrets of Nordstrom's All-Time Top-Performing Salesperson

A salesman minus enthusiasm is just a clerk.

—Harry F. Banks

Before he retired in 2001, Patrick McCarthy was Nordstrom's all-time top salesman, after a 30-year career with the company. For 15 consecutive years, the native of Seattle was the Number One salesman throughout the entire chain.

McCarthy had arrived at Nordstrom from an unlikely place—the state prison in Shelton, Washington, a timber community 60 miles south of Seattle, where he worked as a counselor for felons. The first couple of years at Shelton, he helped adult criminals make the transition to the community by placing them in jobs; after that, he became supervisor of a halfway house for juveniles, counseling them to stay in school or find employment, rather than remain dependent on the state. The work was frustrating and mentally draining.

"I've always believed in hard work, but in that environment, it just wasn't there," recalled McCarthy. "You couldn't get the kid to listen, to understand that you can make something of your life. As much as I wanted to help, I couldn't."

A college friend set up an interview for McCarthy with the friend's father-in-law, Lloyd Nordstrom, one of the three co-chairmen of what was then a seven-store retail chain that generated annual sales of about $80 million, as well as hundreds of new career advancement opportunities. Lloyd Nordstrom advised McCarthy to try a career in sales, a field that McCarthy thought he "might have an aptitude for, because I had always been comfortable with people and sensitive to their feelings."

In January 1971, at the age of 26, with a wife and three young children to support, he joined the men's furnishings and sportswear departments at the store in the Bellevue Square shopping mall, across Lake Washington from Seattle. (At that point, Nordstrom had been selling men's wear for only three years.)

Nordstrom, then as now, provided little in the way of formal sales training. After teaching new employees how the cash register worked, Nordstrom dispatched them to the sales floor to learn about the merchandise and start selling. Although they were paid an hourly wage, the real money (and the scorecard for career advancement) was in high sales commissions.

"I immediately saw that sales were pretty important to these guys. So, that was what I was going to give them," McCarthy recalled, with a touch of understatement.

Unfortunately, he was ill prepared for the job.

"I made every mistake in the book. Although I liked to dress well, I knew virtually nothing about clothing and had no personal style. I wore my shirts too big. I didn't know how to fold garments for display or to coordinate colors and textures. Worse, because I had some learning disabilities, including dyslexia, my work habits and organizational skills were poor. I couldn't even get to work on time."

After three days on the job, McCarthy's sales per-hour track record (the company's standard of performance) was near the bottom of his department.

McCarthy realized that he needed a mentor to teach him how to survive at Nordstrom. He found his role model in a coworker named Ray Black, who was a professional men's wear salesman, who showed McCarthy how to work with the customer. (Black's influence as McCarthy's mentor is explained in detail in Chapter 8.)

Becoming a Team Player

After working at Nordstrom for less than two years, McCarthy came within a thread of being fired because he had developed a reputation for being uncooperative, hard to manage, and not a team player.

McCarthy often found himself discouraged and stuck in what he called a "poor me" attitude. "I'd ask myself, 'Why am I doing all this? Am I making a difference?'" Fortunately, the new men's wear department manager, who had been ordered to terminate McCarthy, didn't believe in dropping the ax without first forming his own opinion. Besides, he'd been told that McCarthy was a sincere man, who was open and friendly with customers and possessed the potential to be a good Nordstrom sales associate.

That department manager, Patrick Kennedy, told McCarthy to stop fighting with coworkers over customers—even at those times when McCarthy was positive that the customer was his. "Ring up the sale for the other guy," said Kennedy, "and smile when you do it."

Then he gave McCarthy some of the most important advice a sales associate can get, advice that McCarthy carried with him ever since, advice that he later gave as a mentor to new employees: "Relax. Stop worrying about making sales."

Easier said than done, thought McCarthy, in the hotly competitive Nordstrom arena of commission sales. But, Kennedy explained, when you stop worrying about money and concentrate on serving the customer, the money will follow. People who succeed in sales understand this paradox.

McCarthy followed Kennedy's advice, and he was able to hone his sales skills. Six months after almost firing McCarthy, Kennedy (who became one of Nordstrom's top corporate footwear merchandisers, and one of McCarthy's best friends), invited McCarthy to become his assistant manager in the men's wear department in a new store that Nordstrom was opening in Yakima, Washington, about 120 miles east of Seattle. McCarthy accepted the offer because it was an opportunity to help create an operation and watch it grow. (Nordstrom had already been operating a shoe store there for several years.) Yakima, which had a small middle-class population (then Nordstrom's primary market), would be his litmus test.

Business was good on the Friday the Yakima store opened and continued at a respectable pace throughout the rest of the weekend, but by Monday the customers had stopped coming in.

"At the end of the day, Pat Kennedy and I found ourselves leaning on the balcony overlooking the selling floor, watching the cosmetic saleswomen put their merchandise away and wondering what we were going to do," McCarthy recalled. "We each had a family to support, and Nordstrom didn't pay us much in those days."

They took matters into their own hands. To generate traffic, McCarthy and Kennedy turned to one of the most basic tools for generating sales: *cold calls*. The two Pats and their wives, Gretchen McCarthy and Judy Kennedy, each seized a telephone book and a telephone and proceeded to call the local doctors, attorneys, automobile dealers, bank presidents, and anyone else who might be in the market for a nice suit.

"Whenever we got a positive reception, we sprang into action," said McCarthy. "Whatever our customers wanted, we obliged. We met them at their office for special fittings. We visited their homes to help them take an inventory of their wardrobe. We told them what to keep and what to discard. Their wives were so appreciative, they would tell us, 'I've been trying to tell him to get rid of that double-knit suit for five years.' We'd start them out with the basics—traditional gray flannel suit and navy blazer, a couple of white shirts, a couple of blue shirts, and maybe a pinstripe. We'd finish off the wardrobe with rep ties, argyle socks, a reversible belt, and a pair of tassel loafers."

Becoming a Super Salesperson

His Yakima experience represented McCarthy's first real steps toward becoming a super salesperson. He began developing his first personal customer book. As we described in Chapter 10, one of the most valuable tools that Nordstrom gives its salespeople is the personal customer book, which helps them keep track of every customer's name, telephone number, charge account number, sizes, previous purchases, vendor preferences, likes and dislikes, special orders, and any other characteristics, such as being a difficult fit or preferring to shop during sales events. They also contain daily, weekly, and monthly calendars, a to-do list, and the phone extension for every department in every Nordstrom store in the country.

The personal books used to be expandable, loose-leaf personal books; today, they are a software program designed for use on a personal computer.

Using his personal book, McCarthy developed the habit of calling specific customers whenever special merchandise came into the store. When birthdays or anniversaries were coming up, he phoned his customers' wives or children with potential gift suggestions.

"Finding My Bliss"

After four months in Yakima, McCarthy tried his hand at being a department manager in another Nordstrom store. But after about a year and a half, he discovered that management wasn't for him because it took him away from sales, while sales took him away from managing. He decided to devote himself exclusively to sales, although, initially, the decision was a blow to his ego because a part of him still coveted the status and cachet of the title of *department manager.* "And after all, doesn't society teach us that management is the ultimate goal?" McCarthy said rhetorically. "To be 'just a salesperson' doesn't sound quite enough, does it? But it was for me. The farther I got away from my management responsibilities, the more I realized that I made the right decision. Sales was what I was good at and felt comfortable with. I was, in the words of the philosopher Joseph Campbell, 'finding my bliss.'"

But even when he reached a point where he felt comfortable as "just a salesperson," McCarthy's sales-education process had barely begun. Despite his extensive experience and the lessons he had learned, it wasn't until he had worked for Nordstrom for seven years that, in his own assessment, his skills "finally came together and my business really started to take off."

McCarthy carried on the tradition of his mentor, Ray Black. Not only was McCarthy famous for his ability to remember names, sizes, and preferences, but also for his empathy, because sometimes his professional relationships with customers can progress to the profoundly personal. McCarthy, who lost his thirteen-year-old son in a fatal accident, is a sympathetic listener, whether counseling a customer whose child needed help kicking a drug habit or advising another customer on what to do with his life after retirement. "This job is more than selling clothes," he said. "It's important for me to give back to the bucket of life."

Among successful Nordstrom people, such a selfless attitude is more the rule than the exception.

Creating a System

You will have noticed that at Nordstrom the priority is on selling. But the key to selling is providing outstanding customer service. Nordstrom's best associates have learned how not to "walk" a customer—that is, not to lose a sale because they couldn't satisfy what the customer wanted. That knowledge comes from practice, experience, and a professional commitment.

As his career grew, McCarthy built his business on referrals. That made it even more essential for him to record all customers' purchases in his personal book because he serviced so many downtown Seattle businessmen. At one point, his client list included 40 lawyers in a downtown Seattle firm of 150 lawyers.

"I had to make sure that two men who work in the same office, or who were likely to run into each other, weren't wearing the same outfit," he said. "You can have as many customers as you want, but you have to take care of each one on an individual basis. Ninety percent of your new clients come from referrals from current clients who appreciate the job you have done. I didn't want to disappoint them by giving bad service."

McCarthy recommends that a new sales associate begin to develop his or her customer service style by starting with the basics: organize and build a system, believe in it, and then execute it. "It's more than thinking positive," said McCarthy. "Positive thinking comes from following simple steps that produce results."

Starting the Work Day

He compared his personal system of customer service to a car engine, whose parts can be taken apart and reassembled.

"I worked hard at not having to look like I was working hard. That came from constantly thinking and planning. I kept on improving as a salesperson because I kept on learning better ways to service the customer. When Larry Bird played basketball, he looked so natural, you would think he must have always played with such skill and confidence. But Larry Bird was once clumsy; he had to work hard to make his play look natural. Larry Bird 'saw' the basketball floor; I 'saw' the sales floor."

McCarthy's preparation for the sales day started virtually with his initial waking thought.

"First put yourself in the right frame of mind. I would look in the mirror and say, 'Okay, Pat, what do you need to do today? Why are you going to work today, and what do you hope to gain?'"

He would arrive at work early to make sure pickups were ready for a customer's arrival. So, when the customer came into the store, McCarthy would not waste time "fumbling around" looking for the customer's purchase.

He used the extra time before the store opened to tackle the most difficult tasks first, so they weren't hanging over his head all day.

"Don't put things off until the end of the day when you're ready to leave. If I had to call a customer because something wasn't done right, I'd get it out of the way. By doing so, I could start the day fresh and the customer got the sense that Nordstrom values and cares for its customers. I was not only building Nordstrom's business, I was building my business and my relationship with that customer."

Once McCarthy arrived in his department at the downtown Seattle store, he was completely focused on the chores of the day. He usually skipped lunch and took no breaks. He always had several projects in progress because "when I was in motion, I was much more creative and opportunities were constantly opening up for me. I visualized my tasks completed. I was continually writing notes, and reviewing the things I had to do for the day, and double-checking to make sure they got done. One list, for example, might consist of things to get done in the tailor shop; another list consists of people to call. Everywhere I turned, there was something being accomplished. I didn't leave things to chance. Things that I planned a week or a month ago were being taken care of. I wanted to do them right the first time so that I would be free to move on to the next task."

At the end of the day, McCarthy, like many associates wrote his thank-you notes so he could start the next day with a clean slate.

"I hated to start up first thing in the morning, so I liked to make sure that there was nothing left to be done at the end of the day," said McCarthy. "Whatever wasn't done was the first item on my list for the next day. Before I went on vacation, I set it up so that I was busy the first week I return. It was like I never left."

Telephone Skills

During the course of his day, he would make about 40 calls to customers. In March, he made calls to alert people to what is coming in for spring. In August, he talked about clothes that would be coming into the store in the fall.

"How to use the telephone and how not to is so important, yet so misunderstood," said McCarthy. "Listen to what your client is asking. Avoid sounding preoccupied; sound like you are devoted to your job and are at the service to the customer. Give him a warm hello—even if you don't feel it. If you are short with him, you are sending the wrong message. It's okay to acknowledge that you are human: 'I've had a terrible morning. Let me get some business out of the way and I'll call you back so that I can devote my full attention to you.'"

McCarthy found that his phone calls provided him with valuable information.

"I saw economic recessions coming six months before the economists did because I could hear it in my customers' voices and saw it in their buying patterns. When business is tough, people buy for needs, not wants. With that information, when I made my next call, I let the customer know that I understood that today might not be the right time to come in, and that I'll touch base in another month or two. But, I want him to know I'm thinking about him."

Product Knowledge

Another way for sales associates to earn the confidence of their customers is to be well versed in the merchandise they sell. When stocking merchandise, McCarthy used the time to memorize which colors, sizes, and manufacturers were available.

Before setting foot onto the selling floor, all Nordstrom sales associates spend time working in the stockroom so that they are thoroughly acquainted with the merchandise, the differences between manufacturers, and, perhaps most importantly, where to find the merchandise in the store.

Associates are encouraged to not only try on the merchandise they sell (in order to experience how it feels) but to buy it and wear it themselves. (McCarthy, generally preferred to wear a traditional two-button suit, plain shirt, and regimental-stripe tie, because "most men want their clothing salesman to dress in the middle of the road, and my job was to receive people; not to intimidate them.")

Dealing with Customers

Working at Nordstrom, McCarthy said, "forces you to deal with everybody: the good the bad, and the ugly. When a customer came into the department on the defensive or had his own opinions, I gave him plenty of room and the opportunity to look over the department on his on. But I still told him that, 'I am here to help you in any way that I can.' The most aggravating customer is the one who doesn't know what he wants and can't reach a decision. I try to get him into a mood where something positive could happen. I might compliment him on the way he dresses and then suggest a manufacturer with a similar style. Or I might comment that the shading of a particular suit would go well with the color of the shoes he was wearing."

While he was on the sales floor as "the Larry Bird of men's wear," McCarthy assumed that "every man who comes into the store hates the idea of shopping for clothes and would rather be somewhere else. When he walked into my department for the first time he was surrounded by an invisible wall. My job was to penetrate that wall. I needed to be relaxed and unhurried so that I could help him feel the same way. I'm not happy until I've created a sense of peace for me and the people around me."

As McCarthy looked for a way to "engage, then disarm," the customer, body language became very important. He would establish eye contact to let the customer know that he was aware of the customer's presence. Like other Nordstrom salespeople, McCarthy would welcome the customer as if he were a guest in

McCarthy's home, and ask: "How are you doing today? You look like you have a question."

"I tried to get started by finding out how things are, what's going on," he explained. "At the same time, I walked him over to his size in a sport coat or slacks and found out what color we needed. Do we need a navy suit or a gray suit? Once we get him in the right size, we look at, specifically, what he is after, so that we are moving in the right direction, so that the time I spend with him is of value to him because he needs to get back to work. I needed to recognize that so that, in the time we have, we can find him a suit or a couple of suits."

If the customer said he was looking for a navy blue suit, for example, McCarthy would escort him over to where that merchandise was displayed. Fit and color were McCarthy's first considerations. He would venture an educated guess on the customer's size to "establish that I'm an experienced professional who knows his business."

Bonding with the Customer

McCarthy would then suggest the customer try on a coat to make sure they had the right size.

"By doing that, we would begin to bond."

Bonding is essential. McCarthy is 6′5″ tall, so he took special care to identify with the customer, not to overpower him. If the customer was short and commented, "I bet you don't have too many suits in my size," McCarthy would counter with: "I bet we have fewer suits in my size than in yours."

In making that quip, McCarthy was "telling him that he's not an oddball. In fact, I may be odder than he is. But the important thing is that we have established a connection."

Throughout the process, McCarthy would casually interview the customer because the "more information you have, the better you can work. What kind of business is he in? What kind of clothes does he wear for business?"

After showing him a selection of suits, McCarthy liked to suggest that the customer browse on his own for a minute or two.

"It's like pheasant hunting. I don't want the dog to flush the bird too quickly," said McCarthy. "I want to let the customer settle down and then move around the department with some freedom. When he's ready, I'll be there to catch him."

Keep the Process Simple

It's imperative to keep the process simple and easy by helping the customer eliminate the things he doesn't want and reducing the number of the options down to two or three.

"You cause confusion when you keep throwing things in and throwing things out until the customer is overloaded," he explained. "Let's not make this brain surgery; this is simple stuff." McCarthy demonstrated his product knowledge by explaining the difference in fabrics, tailoring, and so on, and why particular colors or cuts or manufacturers are more flattering on one customer than on another.

Price is never the primary issue for top Nordstrom sales performers. McCarthy never liked to talk about price.

"The customer tells you that as you go along," he said. "My responsibility was to make sure that the customer saw the best merchandise, so that's where we started. If a suit fit well, but was out of his price range, I'd say, 'Let me show you the next best thing in terms of look.' But I explained why he wasn't going to get as much at the lower price. I reminded him that we all have stuff around the house that we wish we had never bought, and that we would have been happier if we had paid a little more for something that would last. If the suit fit, that's great. But, if he had a problem with the fit in the shoulder or with the collar, it wouldn't look good and I wouldn't feel good about selling it. I didn't want him coming back in a month or two, saying he didn't like it. I would tell him that if, at some point, we could get him into the better-fitting suit, I would feel a lot better about it because I would feel that I was giving him the service he deserved.

"Throughout the process, I constantly asked for his feedback on how the sleeves look and if the coat was cut the way he liked," said McCarthy. "The more information I have, the better sales-man I can be and the better I can serve the customer. I wanted to make sure that we were on the same page and that he had an investment in the decision-making process. This wasn't just my deal. It was not an 'I' experience; it was a 'we' experience. With some customers, I needed to plant the idea in their minds and let them think it over. Two weeks or a month later, a customer would come back as if it was his idea."

Multiple Sales

At Nordstrom, with its commission-oriented culture, the ability to consistently generate multiple sales is the trait that distin-guishes the top sales performers such as McCarthy.

He alerted customers of upcoming sales, gaps in their wardrobes, shoes that need replacement, and ties that bring life to an old suit. McCarthy taught them that clothes convey a look and that maintaining that look is a comprehensive effort. It was not uncommon to see McCarthy walking a customer from men's suits to several other departments to sell him other things.

McCarthy would end his first contact with a new customer by saying something like: "This was fun for me. Shall we do this again?" At that point, they swapped business cards.

McCarthy was able to consistently sell over a million dollars a year because he could handle several customers at one time.

"If another customer came in while I was working with someone else, I would say, 'Hello Tom, I'll be right with you. I'm just finishing up here.' I've acknowledged and recognized him and he knows I'll get back with him. If I'm taking care of another customer at the same time, I'll tell 'Tom' that he has the time to make some decisions. If he needs a pair of slacks, I just get him a pair of slacks. It's a way of transition. You give him attention at the time he needs it, and you give him time to digest what it is he has seen. Or, if he has already made a decision, I will put him into the dressing room, making sure the tailor knows, specifically, what we talked about in terms of fit."

The Sale Is Never Over

The end of the sale was the time for solidifying and bonding.

"This was a very critical moment for me in selling—to make sure that I was planting the seeds for the next time we get together. We are finished with fall shopping now, but there would be things coming up. For example, I would ask him if he was going to be taking a vacation in February or March, so he might need a summer-weight coat and a couple of pairs of pants. If a customer came in to have a suit retailored, I would ask him if he really needed a suit, because he was already in good shape with suits. That would cause him to rethink things and then say, 'Maybe I could use a sport coat.'

"My job was to listen to the customer, to make sure that when that customer walked out that door, he was satisfied. So when I called him again, I didn't want to have to start off the conversation with him saying that he didn't like the suit that I sold to him. I was there to help the customer make the choice but, if he decided that he wanted to go in another direction, I wanted him to understand what he bought and why he bought it. So, if he brought it back, it was not because he didn't know why he bought it. I don't hear salesmen telling that to their customer because they are happy to get the sale, happy to move on to another customer. They don't see the relationship that will last for a long period of time. People today, don't see themselves in the job very long.

"Part of the unsaid, tacit contract is to listen to the customer. As I wrapped up the sale, I reviewed with the customer what he would need to have done next. He would affirm if I was correct. He listened to me and I listened to him. Then I would ask, 'Is there anything else you need?'"

McCarthy didn't limit himself to selling just a suit. "I wanted to make sure that the customer left with everything he needed. Based on what the customer told me, I would suggest other things he might purchase while he was in the store: shirts, ties, underwear, belts, socks, and so on, because *the sale is never over*."

Keys to Success

- Be a team player.
- When you stop worrying about money and concentrate on serving the customer, the money will follow. Successful salespeople understand this paradox.
- Knowledge comes from practice, experience, and professional commitment.

(Continued)

(Continued)

- Positive thinking comes from following simple steps that produce results.
- Create your own system.
- Listen to what the customer is saying.
- Constantly ask for feedback; the more information you have, the better salesperson you will be.
- Engage, then disarm, the customer.
- Keep the process simple.
- The sale is never over.

EXERCISE

Create Your Own System

Assuming that you are empowered by your employee to do whatever it takes to take care of the customer, how do you create your own system within the larger system?

- List the duties and requirements of your job.
- List the choices you have that will help you take care of the customer.
- List the options you have that will best fit you, your personality, and how you like to do business.
- List the reasons for those options and how they can work for both you and your organization.

EXERCISE

Get Feedback from the Customer

The more information you get from your customer the more able you are to take care of your customer.

- Make a list of the choices your organization offers your customers.

- Make a list of all the questions you can ask your customer in order to better understand your customer's needs.

- Compare and combine your list with those of your colleagues. Then come up with a master list of the best series of questions to promote the best in customer service.

12

Play to Win

Encourage Teamwork and Team Competitions at Every Level of Your Organization

One hand cannot applaud alone.

—Arabian Proverb

The Nordstrom Way is a fascinating combination of individual achievement and teamwork.

Nordstrom employees are judged on three criteria: customer service (of course), sales (this is a results-oriented company), and teamwork. The company constantly emphasizes the fact that teamwork is just as important as the other two yardsticks. You can be the highest grossing salesperson in the organization, but if you don't give great service to both the customers and your colleagues, you will not endure at Nordstrom. Consequently, a Nordstrom employee must be a team player.

"Competition is a key element of our culture," explained President Blake Nordstrom. "If done right, a commission incentive system encourages better service and team play. If you are part of our team, the number one thing you have is your integrity, character, and reputation, which you associate with your manager, your store, whatever it might be. You have a vested interest in the success of this company. So, if you see that something is not right, you will speak up and make it right. By doing things properly, you will gain through reputation and financially. It requires constant vigilance."

Constant vigilance is required because, as one might expect, Nordstrom's emphasis on generating high sales occasionally leads a handful of employees to try to find ways of rigging the system or outmaneuvering their fellow employees.

For example, in 2003, the corporate shoe department ran a one-day sales contest among all the shoe departments in all the Nordstrom stores in the chain—a popular motivational device at Nordstrom. The rules were simple: $500 would be awarded to every member of the individual department that sold the most pairs of a particular brand of shoes. In addition, employees received $5.00 for each pair of that brand that they sold. But a small number of salespeople at the downtown Seattle store manipulated the contest. They sold shoes to each other and rang up sales for coworkers, family members, friends, and customers—with the full knowledge that a few days after the contest was over, the shoes would all be returned—thanks to Nordstrom's unconditional, no-questions-asked return policy. But Nordstrom's internal security systems noted an unusually high volume of returns on the brand in question, as well as a high number of incidents of employees ringing up sales for themselves, which by itself is cause for termination. After an internal investigation, 8 of the 17 employees in the department were fired.

Despite this kind of behavior, Nordstrom's top sales performers wouldn't change the commission-oriented, goal-oriented system because competition—both external and internal—stokes the competitive fires at Nordstrom, as well as every other great customer-service organization.

Finding the right balance between rewarding individual achievement, as well as teamwork and customer service, is the key to success.

Individual Achievement

Since the early 1950s, all Nordstrom employees on the sales floor have earned the lion's share of their compensation from sales commissions. Nordstrom empowers and encourages its salespeople to take ownership of their business and to build it up into a thriving enterprise. To help those salespeople succeed, the company gives them the necessary tools—inviting stores, lots of merchandise, thank-you notes, state of the art inventory and replenishment systems, computerized personal books, and so on—and expects them to use those tools to create their own business.

And as we have seen, the company honors and publicizes and rewards its top sales performers through designations such as Corporate Pacesetter All-Star. These people lead by example. They are efficient with their time; they cultivate long-term relationships with customers; they take initiative; they demonstrate their product knowledge; and they set and achieve their goals through outstanding selling skills.

Mentoring, a key aspect of the Nordstrom Way is built on the pillars of teamwork and unselfishness. Top salespeople are encouraged to pass on the information they learned from their mentors. That is how a customer-service, sales-oriented culture is perpetuated and sustained.

Take for example, Bob Bullard, a million-dollar salesperson in the men's wear department at the Corte Madera store in California. A coworker, Kathy Weibel, wrote the following story about Bullard in the Nordstrom employee publication, *The Loop:*

> Bob is a true team player who gives A+ customer service to his clients, his coworkers' customers, and all of us who work in the store. He is always smiling, knows his merchandise, and helps educate us and our customers, too. He jumps right in and cheerfully helps when someone from our team looks "confused" about an upcoming appointment. Bob never assumes that he should receive part of the commission for helping—and he does so much. . . .

Recently a couple called on a Saturday afternoon. The wife needed an outfit for a wedding that they were going to attend. I called to get her information, and she asked if we could also help fit her husband for a suit. She mentioned that he had recently become partially disabled and was in a wheelchair.

When the couple arrived, all of the sizes I had pulled for the husband were wrong because his disabilities were more extensive than I had understood. Not certain how to handle the situation, I called Bob and he immediately came up with someone from the tailor shop. He knew how to fit the customer's very narrow shoulders while still making the trousers work. Bob spoke with the gentleman and understood his challenges. He made him comfortable and sold him two suits with all the accessories. The wife bought her outfit from me, and the two of us had $5,600 in sales.

But the best part was Bob's dedication to making sure everything was right for the couple. The wife had tears of joy in her eyes when they left.

This is a perfect example of the company's striving to strike a balance of customer service, teamwork, and individual achievement. The two Nordstrom employees gave the husband and wife a positive customer service experience, they worked well together and they made a sale: win, win, win.

As mentioned earlier, in the Nordstrom culture, this story is called a *heroic* and they play a critical role in the culture. Employees who witness a colleague giving customer service above and beyond the call of duty are encouraged to write up a description of what they saw or experienced and submit it to their managers, who will publicly praise that employee. The best heroic stories are printed in the Nordstrom employee publication.

What Does Teamwork Look Like?

Teamwork takes many forms at Nordstrom. Sometimes it's subtle, other times it's obvious.

A customer wrote a letter to the company to commend the special service she had received on a visit to the Nordstrom store at the Mall of America. It wasn't just any day; it was her wedding day. The customer had forgotten to pack a few items, her maid of honor needed to buy a dress. The two women had rushed to take the hotel shuttle to the mall and had about an hour before they would have to return, in order to get to the church on time.

The harried customer and maid of honor were greeted by Catherine Behrendt, a salesperson in the Mall of America store, who was apprised of the situation and the time constraints involved. Catherine, wrote the customer in a letter to Nordstrom management, "became part of our team and assisted us in finding a gorgeous dress." She then escorted the two women to the shoe department, where she handed them off to salesperson Joseph Devine.

Meanwhile, Behrendt brought over earrings to complement the dress as they decided on the right shoes. They purchased two pairs. "As if this were not enough," concluded the letter, "Catherine enlisted the assistance of your store concierge to find the name and location of a mall merchant from whom we could buy silk flowers."

That is teamwork.

Of course, the two salespeople in the previous story earned commission money on those sales. But sometimes the most impressive examples of teamwork occur when salespeople don't earn a commission, when those salespeople selflessly go out of their way for the greater good of their department or their store or their region or their company—or just because it makes them feel good.

Take the example of David Simmons, who sells women's shoes in the Florida Mall store in Orlando. Before moving to Orlando, David worked at the Montgomery (Maryland) Mall. One of his old customers from that store had been searching for a pair of the popular UGG boots, but without any success; the boots were virtually impossible to find. The customer decided to contact David to see if he could locate a pair for her because, she wrote in a letter to Nordstrom, she knew that, "If they existed at a Nordstrom store anywhere, David would find them! He is the most ambitious, eager-to-please and pleasant salesperson I have ever had."

Simmons advised the customer that it would be next to impossible to find the boots, but he told her, he "welcomed the challenge." For about a week, he checked the computer daily and called various stores in California, where he had gotten a lead that they were getting some in. He kept the customer updated throughout the entire process. Within days, the pair of UGG boots she was after was on its way from California.

"Not only that, he suggested I call the store and give them my information and have them shipped directly to me, even though he would not get any commission," wrote the customer. "I think he was as excited as I was to find the boots!"

Of course, demonstrating that kind of service to the public is easier to do when you're dealing directly with the customer. What about your employees who almost never see or come in contact with a customer? These people often don't see the connection between what they do and how they impact the customer experience. Nordstrom is creative in finding ways to honor and single out people in support positions.

An example of how nonsales personnel can show their commitment to customer service is the "White Glove Contest," a

Nordstrom tradition for decades, which gives cash rewards and honors to Housekeeping/Maintenance departments that keep their stores clean and inviting to the customers. As Nordstrom management points out in the newsletter to employees, "A store can't win this award unless everyone is involved."

Team Accomplishments

It is essential to reward team accomplishments.

Each year, the company gives the President's Cup to the stores that have achieved the biggest increase in comparable store sales over the past year. The contest highlights three winners every year, depending on the sales volume of the store. As an added bonus, one of the three Nordstrom brothers—Blake, Peter, or Erik—makes an appearance in the winning store, and presents the store employees with a cash prize.

In addition, over the course of the year, individual departments, stores, and regions are recognized for outstanding sales and customer service. Again, these awards help to foster the importance of the team—while being fueled by the performance and success of individuals.

"Selling is a team effort," said salesperson Leslie Umagat. "Our success hinges on the support of other salespeople and management and support staff. You have to be grateful on a consistent basis for your entire team."

Teamwork Breeds a Sense of Ownership

Creating a sense of ownership among employees is key to teamwork.

When Rita Noguchi became manager of a women's apparel department at the Arden Fair store in Sacramento, California, there had been a lot of turnover in the department. "So my number one goal was to make sure we had stability," she said. "Once you have stability and happy people, you can create ongoing customer relationships, and that's how your business grows."

To instill a sense of ownership in her team, Rita decided to divide the responsibility in the department. She assigned each person an area of accountability, such as customer service, new accounts, and developing personal trade.

One salesperson took the responsibility for new accounts. She made a chart to monitor each employee's progress, encouraged her teammates, and awarded prizes to those who signed up the most new accounts. The team rose to number one in new accounts for the Arden Fair store, even though they are one of the store's smallest departments.

Taking this approach, "made the department more fun, because each person knew she could make an impact," said Rita Noguchi. "We continually challenge each other every day to be better."

The teamwork boosted the department's spirit and, as a result, the department soon racked up the number one sales-per-hour increase in the company.

At Nordstrom, when it comes to building positive team relationships, employees are expected to know, understand, and support team goals, and to cooperate with—and show respect for—their coworkers throughout the company.

Nordstrom constantly reinforces the idea that when the company is at its best, it is the result of a group effort. Nordstrom is both a collection of individuals and a seamless team, with each member of that team expected to be ready, willing, and able to take care of each other, while taking care of the customer.

Teamwork cannot be achieved without ethical behavior. Earlier in this chapter, we noted an abuse of the system by a handful of unethical employees who tried to win a sales contest. And we saw how Nordstrom dealt swiftly with those employees. In its training, Nordstrom constantly reinforces the importance of ethical behavior, and spells out what the company demands from its employees, specifically honesty, integrity, and consistency in all their actions.

A recent example of this kind of ethical, unselfish team-oriented behavior happened in a women's apparel department at the Nordstrom store in Bellevue Square, across Lake Washington from downtown Seattle. Salesperson 1 had sold a customer six sweaters, all in the same style, in different colors. The customer, who was about to go away on vacation, tried on the sweaters and found they were the wrong size. Because she was leaving the following day, she took the sweaters back to Bellevue Square to exchange them for the right size. Salesperson 1 was off that day, so the customer told her story to Salesperson 2, who found that the store was out of the customer's size. Salesperson 2 called several Nordstrom stores in the area and found that the sweaters were in the downtown Seattle store. She personally drove to Seattle—a 20- to 30-minute drive with moderate traffic—to pick up the sweaters and brought them back to Bellevue Square.

Who received the commission on the sale of those sweaters?

Salesperson 1, who made the original sale.

Who was a great team player?

Salesperson 2, who did not try to record the sale for herself, but made sure that the sale went to Salesperson 1. And you know that the next time Salesperson 1 has an opportunity to reciprocate, she will, because that's the way teamwork should be done the Nordstrom Way.

Teamwork across Departments, Business Units, and Geography

Nordstrom believes that teamwork brings individuals closer together and helps different departments gain a better understanding of each other's role within the company.

So many organizations face the challenge of creating—and sustaining—relationships with other departments. Without a relationship, it is difficult to understand how the success of that department has an impact on the success of your department.

In this era of multi-channel service—where organizations can do business with their customers either through their brick-and-mortar operations, web site, mail, or telephone—companies are learning how best to coordinate these individual business units.

At Nordstrom, Nordstrom Direct, a division that has one direct fulfillment center, in Cedar Rapids, Iowa, handles customer orders from the company's mail-order catalogs and from its web site. The Nordstrom Direct distribution facility is set up differently than those of the full-line stores (the large Nordstrom stores, as opposed to the smaller Nordstrom Rack discount stores), because each business unit has its own considerations and requirements. But they also, at times, must work together.

"In Direct, our fulfillment center is all automated and picks and packs the items, whereas the full-line (stores fulfillment) center is more of a manual process," explained Ann Delestine, analyst for the Nordstrom Direct Contact Center. Beginning in holiday 2002, Nordstrom Direct partnered closely with full-line stores, "so we understand each other's systems. I would say the best thing about this relationship is that neither party looks at it as 'Well, it's your customer or it's my customer.' It's always our customers."

Nordstrom urges departments within stores to work with each other for the greater good.

"I really encourage my crew to create relationships with different departments," said Angelica Del Bosque, cosmetics manager at Horton Plaza in San Diego. "Think of all the different customers they have access to that we don't . . . and vice versa. We try to include as many departments in our promotions as possible. During [the Half-Yearly sales], for example, we partnered with Savvy to promote Juicy Tube lip glosses and Juicy Couture jumpsuits. We filled up a huge vase with Juicy Tube lip glosses and put it in their department, and set up a station to let Savvy customers sample our products while they tried on the jumpsuits." Since the cosmetics department doesn't participate in the Half-Yearly sale, Angelica believed her business would have been flat without the promotions, but with a little creative teamwork her team recorded a solid increase.

If a Nordstrom salesperson can't find a particular item in her store that a customer is looking for, she will do a "merchandise check" to find the item at another Nordstrom store, whether it's down the road or across the country.

Carolyn Cohn, who sells the exclusively Nordstrom line of Faconnable women's apparel at the Fashion Valley, San Diego store, developed a long-distance teamwork relationship with Debbie Erbes, a salesperson in another department in the Nordstrom store in Fashion Square, Scottsdale, Arizona. Explained Erbes, "I know Carolyn will bend over backwards for me, and I am reciprocal with her."

For the first few years of their long-distance teamwork, Debbie and Carolyn only knew each other through telephone conversations. Eventually, they had an opportunity to meet in San Diego and subsequently nurtured a close friendship.

"I'd like to develop this kind of relationship with everybody I speak with," said Erbes. "A lot of times when a salesperson from another store calls, I'll say, 'How can I make your day?' They love it."

When one employee conveys that kind of positive feeling of cooperation and teamwork, your organization will be well on its way to giving customer service the Nordstrom Way.

Implementation Lessons from Other Companies

When Gordon Bethune took over Continental Airlines (the then-ailing airline) in 1994, he found a company where a series of previous managements had poisoned the idea of teamwork by playing off employees against each other. He told employees, "The only way we all win is if we take care of all the baggage and all the seating and take off and land on time. That takes teamwork. The gate agents and the flight attendants work together because they only win when the customers wins, which means getting the passengers to their destination on time," Customers measure success very simply: "Did I arrive safely and on time and with my underwear?"

Continental's employees "win" when they place among the top three airlines in on-time arrivals. " 'On-time' drives everything," said Bethune. So, they not only have to make sure the planes arrive at their destination on time, they also have to have a performance record that is as good or better than the competition. Competition in the relatively small airline industry is easy to measure because every month, the government publishes the standings—first place through last place—based on on-time performance, number of bags lost, customer complaints, and so on.

St. Charles Medical Center in Bend, Oregon, has a program called "people-centered" teams that is about relationship training. It's all about "the relationship that we establish with patients, with families, between each other, ultimately determines the clinical outcome of patients," said CEO emeritus Jim Lussier. He often uses this example: "If you're going into our surgery to have your head cut open and have a craniotomy done, would you rather have it done by a team that is fully functioning, that gets along well, that supports each other, and is there for the patient, or one that is constantly, arguing, bickering, having outside affairs. Which do you think will be better clinically?"

Creating that kind of environment is done in a variety of ways. As an example, Lussier cited a staff member, who administers EKG tests. That person and a colleague were trying to do an EKG on a chronically ill child who had been coping with heart defects since her birth.

"They were having a devil of a time getting a good EKG done," Lussier recalled. Nothing was working. "Finally, they sat down with her and sang 'Twinkle, Twinkle Little Star' for a couple of minutes. It worked. They calmed her down, made her feel comfortable, and were able to perform the process. When they were finished, she was happy as a lark. She wasn't forced into a situation that would make her uncomfortable." That's teamwork.

Lussier is an evangelist for customer service in the health care industry, where, "patients as customers is totally foreign," he said. "Would you go into Nordstrom if the first thing they did was stick you in a waiting room and say, 'I'll be back in an hour'?"

At FirstMerit, it's the responsibility of every team member to create a relationship with the customer. All employees involved in selling bank products are assembled as teams and are taught each other's business, including a broad and detailed understanding of the features and benefits of each product and service that a corporate customer would need. They are taught how to identify that need and how to speak to the benefits of that product.

This building up of relationships among and between these employees creates camaraderie and a greater desire to help the group. They know when to smoothly and politely hand off the customer to the FirstMerit service provider who is trained to explain the product in greater detail.

"It's important to build that proper protocol of referral," said FirstMerit CEO John Cochran. "It's equally important for the banker who receives the referral to acknowledge the employee who made it happen. It's just like when someone walks into the clothing department at Nordstrom and buys a suit. The salesperson who sold the customer that suit then takes the customer into another department to sell him shirts and ties and socks. The responsibility of the person who open that line of credit or checking account, and so on is to introduce the customer to the additional services."

For example, a customer told a FirstMerit customer-service representative that he had just been awarded a large monetary claim from an insurance company for a personal injury. The FirstMerit customer-service representative immediately referred the customer to FirstMerit's trust department, where an expert spoke to the customer about the necessity for estate planning.

For all employees—from tellers to branch managers—who come in direct contact with customers, a portion of their compensation is tied directly to their ability to successfully help sell the customer a product that they don't personally sell themselves.

"We thrive on internal competition," said Cochran.

Cochran said the FirstMerit's best personal bankers are the ones who have the best teamwork inside their branches. "They don't see the goal as 'my' goal, but rather 'our' goal. They look for how to help each other achieve their goals. We constantly drive home the point that the customer's experience in the branch is fully owned by the branch and by every employee who works in the branch. That's teamwork."

FirstMerit develops a healthy sense of camaraderie, by offering a variety of categories, including "most improved," where many employees can get a chance to win something. The contests run for specific periods of time, usually six to eight weeks, so they create bursts of energy and focus that generate revenue and build customer relationships that can last all year. Because these contests run for short periods of time, employees know they need to maximize their efforts because they don't know when the next one is going to come.

Individuals have to operate as a team. FirstMerit, which was inspired by Nordstrom's penchant for contests, launched a contest of its own, called "The Best Branch," which include a variety of criteria, including achieving sales quotas, service quality, community involvement, and reports from mystery shoppers. All the categories and criteria are geared toward enhancing the customer experience while meeting performance expectations and revenue goals. Since everyone has a scorecard, all employees know exactly where they stand, and what they need to do in order to create a unique FirstMerit experience. These are team goals for each bank branch, not the goals of individuals.

As Cochran sees, it, "At Nordstrom, the guy who's selling shoes needs the guy selling suits to refer him business. At the end of the day, you're going to figure out that, in order to get good at your job, you need to be cooperative with a fellow team member."

The first edition of this book ended with a quote from John N. Nordstrom of the third generation of Nordstroms, who was interviewed for a corporate video for new employees. This statement by the retired co-chairman, this grandson of founder John W. Nordstrom, remains just as relevant today:

> Our commitment is 100 percent to customer service. We are not committed to financial markets; we are not committed to real estate markets; we are not committed to a certain amount of profit. We are only committed to customer service. If we make a profit, that's great. But customer service is first. If I'm a salesperson on the floor and I know that the people that own this place are committed to customer service, then I am free to find new ways to give great customer service. I know that I won't be criticized for taking care of a customer. I will only be criticized if I *don't* take care of a customer.

Keys to Success

- Find ways to balance individual achievement and teamwork.
- Honor team achievements.
- Show how every team member is important to customer service—even if that team member has no direct contact with the customer.
- Promote teamwork among groups within your organization and find ways for them to compete—on a positive basis—with other teams within your organization.
- At the same time, promote the larger team—your entire organization—in its competition with your rivals.

(Continued)

(Continued)

■ Encourage people to take ownership of customer-service issues.

■ Promote ethical behavior.

■ Promote unselfish behavior.

■ Promote teamwork across all departments, business units, and regional offices.

■ Encourage employees to cite the teamwork example of other employees.

■ Publicize those "heroic" stories of teamwork throughout your organization.

■ Make them part of your value system.

EXERCISE

Team Achievement

Do you honor team achievement within your organization? How can you make team achievement a bedrock of your culture?

■ Assemble a group of people from all departments within your organization. Their assignment is the following:

■ Create categories for team achievement.

■ Devise awards for honoring team achievement.

■ Determine the criteria for winning each award.

■ Determine how each award will be judged.

EXERCISE

Teamwork Requirements

Nordstrom has a list of requirements to promote team goals.

- Assemble a group of people from all departments within your organization. Their assignment is the following:
- Create your own list of requirements for team goals.
- Distribute those requirements to all members of your organization.
- Ensure that those requirements become an essential part of your culture.

EXERCISE

Ethical Behavior

- Assemble a group of people from all departments within your organization. Their assignment is the following:
- Create your own list of ethical behavior guidelines.
- Distribute that list to all members of your organization.
- Ensure that those guidelines become an essential part of your culture.

EXERCISE

Ownership

How can people who don't deal with a customer, feel a sense of ownership of the customer service experience?

- Assemble people in your organization. This group should be comprised of frontline and support staff.

- Brainstorm how support staff can be made to feel a part of the customer service team.

- Design a way for support staff to meet and discuss customer-service issues with your customers.

- Discuss ways that different departments, business units, and regional offices can interact to best serve the needs of your customers.

- Record all those ideas and distribute it to all members of the organization.

- Ask for additional suggestions.

EXERCISE

Heroics

As we have seen, heroics—examples of outstanding teamwork—are a part of the Nordstrom culture.

- Devise ways of encouraging all members of your organization to single out their coworkers for "heroic" stories.

- Find ways to spread these stories throughout your organization.

Appendix

Nordstrom Heroics

Inspirational Tales of Teamwork and Legendary Customer Service

When a Nordstrom employee witnesses a coworker providing great customer service—whether for a customer or a colleague, he or she is encouraged to write up what that coworker has done, and these write-ups are shared with other employees. In the Nordstrom culture, these stories are called *heroics*. Heroics are an essential feature of the Nordstrom Way because they demonstrate and illustrate qualities of teamwork and customer service that ultimately produce sales. They also allow employees to recognize fellow employees for the special lengths they go through for a customer (who may never know what that "heroic" employee did).

By sharing these heroics, Nordstrom management honors and salutes employees who go above and beyond the call of duty, which sends the message that customer service—both internally and externally—is what makes Nordstrom Nordstrom.

The examples of Heroics in this Appendix originally appeared in the Nordstrom employee publication, *The Loop*. (For privacy, names have been omitted.)

Trusting the Customer

An employee from the Easton Town Center store wrote this note praising one of her coworkers:

> Recently, a couple from New Hampshire stopped in Studio 121 and this employee helped them. The wife tried on a red jacket with matching sweater and looked fabulous. Her husband kept telling her to buy them, but she hesitated even though she loved them.
>
> The salesperson questioned the customer about her hesitation. The customer told her they were in from out of town for a party, and she hadn't brought her jewelry. The salesperson asked the customer if she liked the necklace and earrings the salesperson was wearing, and the customer replied yes. The salesperson offered to loan them for the evening. The customer bought the jacket and sweater and when the salesperson wrapped the purchases she also wrapped her jewelry to go with them. The couple was staying close to where the salesperson's son works, so she gave them directions to drop off her jewelry with him. The jewelry was returned along with a very gracious thank you note.

Helping a Cancer Survivor Feel Better about Herself

A manager at a Nordstrom store in Oakbrook, Illinois, wrote up this heroic describing the compassion of a salesperson in her store:

> A customer from Wisconsin has never been to our store and has never seen her salesperson's face. Her Nordstrom cosmetics salesperson helps her entirely by phone. From the beginning, the salesperson did all the right things. She suggested great products, included free samples, went to different cosmetic lines to find products and shipped everything to Wisconsin.

The salesperson has been following through to take care of the customer's needs for about a year.

Sadly, the customer has cancer. A year ago she received her diagnosis and deals every day with the effects of the disease. She has had trouble feeling pretty, has lost her short-term memory and sense of smell, and worries about her husband.

The customer says the service she receives makes a world of difference. She feels beautiful again, and says that her Nordstrom salesperson has been part of her recovery process.

Helping a Customer Through Brain Surgery

An employee at a Nordstrom store in the Washington DC area wrote this Heroic about his coworker:

I'm not sure how the call originated, but this employee helped get an outfit to a man who was having brain surgery at Fairfax hospital. He was traveling from Portland, Maine, and had to have emergency surgery while here in Virginia. She brought him some clothes and learned that his wife had nothing to wear that worked with our climate. She had borrowed clothes from the nurses. So, the salesperson offered to pick her up at the hospital and bring her here to the store to do some shopping. The woman was delighted and found some outfits. The employee returned her to the hospital after her shopping spree.

Stepping in for a Coworker

The manager of a department in a Nordstrom store in Portland, Oregon, wrote this heroic about a salesperson's team spirit, drive, and willingness to serve:

I was apprehensive about leaving my crew for a vacation because of the heavy shipments of anniversary merchandise we were receiving.

This salesperson must have known I was nervous about being gone. He offered to swap shifts with a coworker over the weekend so he would be opening. This would allow him more time to work the merchandise, set the floor, and pull figures.

I was impressed with his confidence as he read my expectations and said, "No problem!" And before I left, he showed initiative by calling me with a suggestion for organizing the stockroom. His ideas saved everyone else a lot of time and energy!

When I returned, the stockroom looked great; there was a pile of figures on my desk for my review, and the jeans were all sized and folded on the back wall. He showed great leadership in stepping up to get things done, and also effectively delegated projects to other crew members. I feel fortunate to have such an amazing person on our floor.

How Support People Provide Customer Service

Organizations often ask how they can get their back-office or support people—employees who rarely, if ever, deal with the customer—to understand the connection between their jobs and taking care of the customer. Here are some examples of how non-salespeople at Nordstrom seized the opportunities to provide great customer service.

The store administrator at a Nordstrom store in Atlanta, Georgia, wrote this Heroic recognizing two employees in Loss Prevention:

These two men are awesome! I know I can always count on them. Last weekend I was expecting a shipment from FedEx that did not arrive on time. I told one of them, and he took the initiative to call FedEx and make arrangements to pick the shipment up at the local station, which happened to be close to where his coworker lived. One of these employees called the other and asked him to pick up the shipment before he got in at 7:00 A.M. on Monday. He arrived with just one box that was smaller than I expected. Apparently, there were supposed to be three boxes. He returned to the FedEx station to retrieve the remaining boxes without question.

These guys are just amazing. Thank you, gentlemen, for taking care of me and the store!

A Nordstrom department manager in the Troy, Michigan, store sent this Heroic to thank the Region's Emergency Response Team for their help during the East Coast Blackout of the summer of 2004:

On behalf of my team, please thank the entire Central States Emergency Response Team for their support and assistance during a challenging time. I will never forget the initial feeling when our power went out. The Somerset Emergency Response Team kicked into action—standing at doors to assist customers and checking dressing rooms, restrooms, and the elevators for distressed customers. Management secured the store while at the same time assisting any customer who wished to continue shopping.

All the members of the our Emergency Response, Loss Prevention, and Maintenance and Housekeeping teams should be commended for their patience and hard work during this hectic crisis.

The promptness and high sense of urgency displayed by the entire region helped us to have light at the end of our tunnel while we were in the dark.

A Customer Service Specialist came to the rescue of a customer in need:

She went above and beyond to help a customer who was traveling in France. The customer was out of money, her ATM card was not working, and she had no place to stay and nothing to eat. Thousands of miles away from home, unable to reach her family and with no resources, the customer contacted her credit card companies, hoping they would temporarily increase her line of credit. None were willing to help her, until she contacted Nordstrom.

Without hesitation, the Nordstrom Customer Service Specialist increased her line of credit so that she would be able to afford food and lodging until her flight back home. The customer said that the Nordstrom employee took care of her like family and that her actions spoke for Nordstrom's uniqueness.

Teamwork, Teamwork, Teamwork

A department manager at a Nordstrom store in New Jersey sent in this heroic recognizing the talents of several employees in the Tailor Shop and Alterations department:

I had a customer who was leaving for Milan the next day. He only wanted a pair of Norsport pants to wear between business meetings. He mentioned that he needed other things, but was going to buy them there because he didn't think it would be possible to get the alterations done in time.

I showed him a lot of things that he might like for his trip—why waste time shopping for clothes on your vacation?

We tried to find pants with exact length sizes, but to no avail. I called a tailor from the Tailor Shop. He graciously agreed to have them done in an hour.

Then the customer needed a jacket. I showed him the washable suede from Newport Harbor. Both he and his wife loved it, but the sleeves had to be shortened. The Tailor Shop was overwhelmed, so I asked Alterations for help. One employee offered to have it done first thing in the morning. The customer was happy to pick it up on the way to the airport. The employee in Alterations asked if someone from the Tailor Shop could just measure the sleeves. One of the tailors came down to measure them agreed to be a hero and do the sleeves before the customer came back for his pants, rather than having Alterations take care of it in the morning.

Three of the customer's shirts also had to be pressed for the trip. I thought I had done enough to bother the guys in the Tailor Shop for the rest of the year, so I proceeded to press them myself. One of the tailors was just finishing pressing some other items, so I asked him to show me how to work the big steamer. He proceeded to do the shirts for me, and wouldn't stop even when I asked him to.

I let the employee in Alterations know that I appreciated her help, but that the Tailor Shop came through and everything was ready for the customer when he returned. He was so pleased, and what was originally a $39.50 sale turned into a $650 sale! Please recognize everyone—they each deserve a special prize for this Heroic.

A salesperson from the Short Hills Mall store sent this letter to Nordstrom President Blake Nordstrom, because she wanted to recognize the lengths her team members went to on her behalf to make sure they did not disappoint a customer.

I am writing to you to let you know the exemplary service experience that I had the pleasure to witness. One crazy Saturday in October, we had a customer call who was supposed to receive a Roberto Cavalli dress overnight for Saturday delivery. She was wearing it to an event that evening and the dress never arrived due to DHL's mistake. The customer was upset as she had purchased shoes and accessories to go with the dress. An employee from the Collectors department, the store manager, and myself sprang into action to try to alleviate this issue for the customer. We went to competitors to see if they possibly had the dress in stock, but no such luck. To make matters worse, it was the last dress of its kind in the collection.

The customer mentioned to the Collectors' salesperson that there was another dress in a boutique in Northern New Jersey (about an hour from the store) that was her second choice to wear to the event, but it needed alterations. The customer said that she had to leave for her event in two hours and there was no way that she would have time to pick it up and have it altered within two hours.

That is when the Short Hills team went into action. The store manager flew out the door to go to the store in northern New Jersey to buy the $2,000 dress for the customer. He then met us at the customer's house. The Norstrom alterations manager agreed to go to the customer's house to do the alterations. The Collectors department salesperson and I drove with the alterations manager to the customer's house with several dresses in tow, just in case the one from the boutique did not work.

We all converged on the customer's house—the store manager with gown in hand, the alterations manager with her needle, and the Collectors department salesperson with her amazing fashion sense to dress the customer head to toe. The alterations manager pinned the gown in the customer's bedroom and then handstitched the hem of the dress at the kitchen counter! We all had such a sense of urgency for this customer and truly wanted her to feel good about what she was wearing to the event.

If that were not enough, the customer's sister was visiting her. The sister was not pleased with her own outfit that she was wearing to the event that night. She tried on one of the gowns that the Collectors department salesperson had brought along and ended up purchasing a $2500 Dolce & Gabbana gown to wear to the event and a $2500 suit that she just had to have as well!

The customers were so pleased that Nordstrom was willing to go to such great lengths just to make her happy. I was so proud to watch such excellent customer service in action. This is what our company was founded on. Please recognize them for this effort.

Saving Christmas

An employee sent this Heroic about the efforts of a department manager on behalf of a child during the holiday season:

> During the holidays, this department manager was "Manager in Charge" for the store. She received a call to go to Santa's Chair and explain to a little girl that Santa wasn't there right now, but would be back the next day. The little girl was about six years old, and told the department manager that she really didn't think her mom could bring her back. The little girl was completely devastated and made the employee promise to personally give her list to Santa. The employee assured her that she would, and even gave the girl her card.
>
> The department manager felt terrible. She could see it was important to the child to give her list to Santa, as he seemed to be her only hope for presents. The child said that if she could only have one thing, she really wanted the Spider Man movie (and maybe a husband for her Mom). This broke the employee's heart.
>
> She showed the list to her husband and suggested they get the movie and send it to the little girl from Santa. Her husband said, "Give me the list. I'm getting it all." They called the girl's mother and made arrangements to give her the best Christmas ever. Another employee's husband drives a tow truck at night, and one evening after the little girl was asleep, they showed up with a tree and all the trimmings and left it on the porch.
>
> Together, this employee and her "elves" made Christmas special for a little girl who wanted nothing more than a video,

a Christmas tree and someone to look out for her mom. Without hesitation or thought for thanks, their actions reminded us that the holidays are a time for making dreams come true.

Wedding Day Wonder

Two employees from the Nordstrom store in Chandler Fashion Center (Arizona) truly went above and beyond for these customers on their special day:

One of the salesperson's personal customers was planning a surprise wedding, full of special personal touches for his fiancée, in her best friend's backyard. Everything from the invitations to the photographer was falling into place—except for somebody to perform the ceremony.

As the day of the wedding drew near, the customer went to his Nordstrom salesperson to have his tux fitted—and it came up in conversation that the salesperson was an ordained minister.

"Does that mean that you could marry us?" the customer asked.

The salesperson said yes.

His department manager happily gave him the time off. The wedding was a phenomenal success, and the customer's bride was happily surprised. The salesperson held up very well under the pressure of meeting family and friends for the first time at the wedding. And the department manager, who is also an artist and owner of his own gallery, invited the happy couple to the gallery to pick out a wedding present. The couple continues to frequent the store as they live happily ever after.

Notes

Nordstrom, Elmer. *A Winning Team: The Story of Everet, Elmer & Lloyd Nordstrom*. Seattle, WA: Dogwood Press,1985.

Nordstrom, John W. *The Immigrant in 1887*. Seattle, WA: Dogwood Press, 1950.

Spector, Robert. *Lessons from the Nordstrom Way: How Companies Are Emulating the #1 Customer Service Company*. New York: John Wiley & Sons, 2001.

Underhill, Paco. *Why We Buy: The Science of Shopping*. New York: Touchstone, 1999.

Index

Index

Index